SpringerBriefs in Applied Sciences and Technology

SpringerBriefs present concise summaries of cutting-edge research and practical applications across a wide spectrum of fields. Featuring compact volumes of 50 to 125 pages, the series covers a range of content from professional to academic.

Typical publications can be:

- A timely report of state-of-the art methods
- An introduction to or a manual for the application of mathematical or computer techniques
- A bridge between new research results, as published in journal articles
- A snapshot of a hot or emerging topic
- An in-depth case study
- A presentation of core concepts that students must understand in order to make independent contributions

SpringerBriefs are characterized by fast, global electronic dissemination, standard publishing contracts, standardized manuscript preparation and formatting guidelines, and expedited production schedules.

On the one hand, **SpringerBriefs in Applied Sciences and Technology** are devoted to the publication of fundamentals and applications within the different classical engineering disciplines as well as in interdisciplinary fields that recently emerged between these areas. On the other hand, as the boundary separating fundamental research and applied technology is more and more dissolving, this series is particularly open to trans-disciplinary topics between fundamental science and engineering.

Indexed by EI-Compendex, SCOPUS and Springerlink.

Fabio Cassia · Paola Castellani · Chiara Rossato
Editors

Accessible Tourism in the Digital Ecosystem

Springer

Editors
Fabio Cassia
Department of Management
University of Verona
Verona, Italy

Paola Castellani
Department of Management
University of Verona
Verona, Italy

Chiara Rossato
Department of Management
University of Verona
Verona, Italy

ISSN 2191-530X ISSN 2191-5318 (electronic)
SpringerBriefs in Applied Sciences and Technology
ISBN 978-3-031-38781-4 ISBN 978-3-031-38782-1 (eBook)
https://doi.org/10.1007/978-3-031-38782-1

This Springer imprint is published by the registered company Springer Nature Switzerland AG
The registered company address is: Gewerbestrasse 11, 6330 Cham, Switzerland

Preface

Accessibility in tourism is attracting growing interest from scholars, firms, not-for-profit organizations, and government organizations. While accessible tourism was previously intended only to satisfy the needs of people with access requirements, there is now a consensus that accessible tourism is beneficial for society at large and that it requires effective co-creation among multiple stakeholders. However, many studies report unsatisfactory levels of coordination and cooperation among the involved stakeholders resulting in low levels of well-being for tourists both with and without access requirements.

To address this gap, this book provides a conceptually and methodologically updated view of accessible tourism, built on the digital ecosystem logic, with the intent of outlining solutions to improve accessible tourism experiences and the accessibility of tourism destinations.

The book begins with a contribution from Baratta and Rossato, providing an overview of the concepts of accessibility and accessible tourism. Vigolo and Simeoni then examine the market for accessible tourism and the related emerging themes, including the dimensions and importance of the accessible tourism market; the importance of the tourist experience; travel motivations; travel constraints; and travel needs. In the next section, Cassia, Bigi, and Ugolini introduce digital ecosystems from both the conceptual and operations perspectives. In particular, they examine how ecosystems support cooperation among actors to remove barriers to accessibility along the tourism journey and to co-create accessible tourism experiences. Castellani and Vargas-Sánchez address accessible tourism from the destination perspective, highlighting the links between smart tourism destinations and accessible tourism. They also discuss the need for and mode of coordination among the destination's actors. The following chapter by Castellani, Bazzani, and Brunetti presents two insightful practical case studies of accessible tourism enabled by digital ecosystems (Alto Adige per Tutti—South Tyrol for All and Hidden Disability Sunflower), outlining the factors at the base of their success. Finally, in the last chapter of the book, Baccarani and Cavallo provide future-oriented reflections to "make accessible tourism happen."

We would like to thank all of our colleagues who contributed to the creation of this book, addressing the multiple facets and implications of accessible tourism. There is no doubt that quick and continuous technological advancements will offer new opportunities to enhance the co-creation of accessible tourism experiences. However, the effective use of new technologies will need to develop in tandem with advancements in actors' awareness of the relevance of accessibility in tourism and their orientation toward cooperation.

Verona, Italy

Fabio Cassia
Paola Castellani
Chiara Rossato

Contents

Contributors

Claudio Baccarani University of Verona, Verona, Italy

Rossella Baratta University of Bergamo, Bergamo, Italy

Francesca Bazzani University of Verona, Verona, Italy

Alessandro Bigi Royal Docks School of Business and Law, University of East London, London, UK

Federico Brunetti University of Verona, Verona, Italy

Fabio Cassia University of Verona, Verona, Italy

Paola Castellani University of Verona, Verona, Italy

Daniela Cavallo University of Verona, Verona, Italy

Chiara Rossato University of Verona, Verona, Italy

Francesca Simeoni University of Verona, Verona, Italy

Marta Ugolini University of Verona, Verona, Italy

Alfonso Vargas-Sánchez University of Huelva, Huelva, Spain

Vania Vigolo University of Verona, Verona, Italy

Chapter 1
Accessibility and Accessible Tourism: The Conceptual Evolution Through the Analysis of the Literature

Chiara Rossato and Rossella Baratta

Abstract The desire for sustainable growth and inclusivity is increasing. Accessibility is a critical feature of inclusion, particularly in tourism, one of the world's largest industries. The purpose of this chapter is to shed light on the conceptual evolution of accessible tourism in the light of technological developments through a review of the literature on the topic. This chapter first presents the theoretical background of the concepts of diversity, inclusion and accessibility in tourism. It then explains the methodology followed for the literature review and presents an analysis of the results. Finally, reflections and future research directions are proposed.

Keywords Diversity in tourism · Inclusive tourism · Dimensions of accessibility in tourism · Sustainable tourism · Role of digital technology

1.1 Introduction

The need for a more sustainable world has become rapidly evident in recent years, reflected in public opinion, civil societies, government activities and scholarly research [1]. To this end, the European Union is promoting the United Nations 2030 Agenda (https://unstats.un.org/sdgs/report/2020/), which identifies 17 Sustainable Development Goals (SDGs) aimed at achieving sustainable growth from economic, social and environmental perspectives. The SDGs are also a response to the pressing need to eliminate barriers and discrimination and integrate multiple forms of diversity to ensure inclusive development.

With respect to the tourism sector, inclusiveness is the cornerstone on which accessibility for all rests. Accessible tourism (AT) is a growing research stream in

C. Rossato (✉)
University of Verona, Verona, Italy
e-mail: chiara.rossato@univr.it

R. Baratta
University of Bergamo, Bergamo, Italy

F. Cassia et al. (eds.), *Accessible Tourism in the Digital Ecosystem*,
SpringerBriefs in Applied Sciences and Technology,
https://doi.org/10.1007/978-3-031-38782-1_1

the tourism literature, motivating researchers and practitioners to outline solutions to make tourist destinations and services more accessible (for all). An important area of research in this regard is new technologies that can drive changes in the tourism sector [2] and strongly affect the competitiveness of tourist destinations [3]. Moreover, these technologies can enable the emergence of a digital ecosystem [4], a relevant resource for AT.

Given the widespread use of technology and the importance of digital accessibility during the COVID-19 pandemic, smart tourist destinations are expected to meet the accessible technology needs of all tourists, allowing them to fully participate in the tourism experience [5, 6]. However, research on the extent to which physical accessibility coincides with digital accessibility is lacking. Thus, the way in which smart destinations integrate accessibility and rethink tourism strategies in terms of both physical and digital dimensions is an emerging research topic and a matter of interest for the effective development of tourist destination accessibility [7].

The aim of this chapter is to review the literature on AT, specifically the role of technology in the evolution of AT and enabling the AT experience during the entire tourism customer journey.

The remainder of this chapter is structured as follows. Section 1.2 provides a theoretical background on the concepts of diversity, inclusion and accessibility in tourism. Section 1.3 explains the methodology used for the literature review. Section 1.4 presents the results of the literature review, and Sect. 1.5 provides a discussion, future research directions and conclusions.

1.2 Theoretical Background

1.2.1 Diversity and Inclusion in Tourism

Diversity and inclusion are becoming increasingly important in contemporary society. The COVID-19 pandemic, in particular, has highlighted the differences between those who are typically included and those who have been traditionally excluded, such as marginalised groups [8]. Diversity has been defined as 'the representation, in one social system, of people with distinctly different group affiliations of cultural significance' [9, p. 5]. Inclusion refers to 'the degree to which individuals feel a part of critical organisational processes such as access to information and resources, involvement in work groups, and ability to influence the decision-making process' [10, p. 48]. Inclusion is also a key step to achieving sustainable development and is one of the central principles of Agenda 2030. According to the United Nations: 'People are excluded from development because of their gender, ethnicity, age, sexual orientation, disability or poverty ... Development can be inclusive—and reduce poverty—only if all groups of people contribute to creating opportunities, share the benefits of development and participate in decision-making'(http://www.undp.org).

Diversity and inclusion are fundamental social requirements for all organisations in modern society [8] and have become increasingly relevant in tourism, one of the world's largest industries. Inclusive tourism has been defined as 'transformative tourism in which marginalized groups are engaged in ethical production or consumption of tourism and the sharing of its benefits' [11, p. 4]. Therefore, inclusive tourism, both from production and consumption perspectives, should be available to all.

Some researchers have explored diversity and inclusion in the tourism and hospitality workforce [12].

However, diversity and inclusion pertain not only to hospitality and tourism employees but also to those who benefit from tourism and hospitality services (i.e., tourists). Moreover, given that travel is a universal right under the Global Code of Ethics for Tourism (http://ethics.unwto.org/en/content/full-text-global-code-ethics-tourism), tourism research should also focus on potential tourists; that is, those traditionally excluded from participation in tourism activities or marginalised because of their 'low socio-economic status, ethnicity, indigeneity, age, gender, sexuality, ability or the intersectionality of the compounding effects of these areas of identity' [13, p. 140]. Given that people are excluded for different reasons (http://www.undp.org), different dimensions of diversity can be identified, including disability, age, gender, ethnicity, religion, socioeconomic status and culture.

Prior research has largely focused on the rights of people with disabilities (PwD) and the urgent need to provide them with opportunities to participate in tourism [e.g., 13, 14]. Moreover, much research attention has been paid to older segments of the population given their economic relevance and special needs [e.g., 15, 16]. With respect to sexual orientation and gender, researchers have studied the inclusion of 'rainbow' [e.g., 17] and LGBTIQ+ tourists [e.g., 18, 19] and the risk perceptions of solo female travellers [e.g., 20]. Moreover, the inclusion of ethnic minorities [e.g., 21] and tourists of different religions [e.g., 22, 23] have been investigated. Other authors have investigated financial inclusion as a means of enhancing tourism demand in emerging economies [24] and for low-income families and other groups who may need financial support to participate in tourism [e.g., 25–27]. Social inclusion has also been investigated through a focus on increasing access to tourism for marginalised groups [28].

AT is a component of inclusive tourism (http://ethics.unwto.org/en/content/accessible-tourism), and, as discussed in the following section, accessibility is a key characteristic of inclusion [29].

1.2.2 *Accessibility in Tourism and Accessible Tourism*

Accessibility is a key component of tourism and tourist destinations. According to Crompton's model of push and pull factors [30], accessibility is a key pull factor attracting visitors to a destination. Several tourism studies [31] have also shown that accessibility is critical for tourist destination competitiveness. In addition, tourism service providers should consider accessibility in terms of both travelling to and after arriving at the destination (e.g., transport, infrastructure, hospitality and services). Accessibility in tourism can be defined as the absence of any kind of barrier—architectural, cultural, sensorial, attitudinal, communicational or informational [32]. Moreover, different dimensions of accessibility exist, including physical accessibility, information accessibility, economic accessibility and psycho-social accessibility (https://ec.europa.eu/docsroom/documents/5568/attachments/1/translations/en/renditions/native).

Given the growing number of people with special accessibility needs [33], tourism researchers have paid increasing attention to the concept of AT [13, 32]. While inclusive tourism focuses on both tourism production and consumption by all types of marginalised groups, AT focuses on enabling access to tourist services and destinations to differently abled people as consumers of tourism [11]. One of the most comprehensive and accepted definitions of AT is provided by Buhalis and Darcy [14, pp. 10–11].

Accessible tourism is a form of tourism that involves collaborative processes between stakeholders that enables people with access requirements, including mobility, vision, hearing and cognitive dimensions of access, to function independently and with equity and dignity through the delivery of universally designed tourism products, services and environments. This definition adopts a whole-of-life approach where people through their lifespan benefit from accessible tourism provision. These include people with permanent and temporary disabilities, seniors, obese, families with young children and those working in safer and more socially sustainably designed environments.

Despite the broad scope of the definition of AT research on the topic has mainly focused on PwD [34]; that is, people with permanent or temporary impairments, activity limitations and participation restrictions. According to the World Health Organization (https://www.who.int/topics/disabilities/en/), 15% of the world's population experiences some kind of disability. Therefore, AT not only refers to equitable tourism but may also offer enormous business opportunities.

Since the United Nations' 1975 Declaration on the Rights of Disabled Persons (https://www.ohchr.org/EN/ProfessionalInterest/Pages/RightsOfDisabledPersons.aspx), tourism researchers have paid increasing attention to AT, and the tourism industry has boosted its efforts to increase the accessibility of tourism destinations and services for all, including those with different forms of disability [35] and from diverse backgrounds. In practical terms, the International Organization for Standardization has launched ISO 21902:2021 [36], a set of requirements and recommendations for tourism destinations and stakeholders to ensure equal tourism access and enjoyment for people of all ages and abilities, building AT for all.

Nevertheless, the tourism industry is still lagging [13]. Therefore, it is of pivotal importance to deepen the analysis to make tourism and tourist destinations truly accessible. The next section examines the relevant role of technology in creating a tourism industry that is effectively and concretely accessible to all.

1.2.3 The Role of Technology in Accessible Tourism

Technology is rapidly evolving, but many studies have failed to consider the role of new technologies in enabling AT experiences. The existing literature is fragmented and mainly identifies technological solutions to accessibility in specific fields such as hospitality, health and communication [37]. For example, Lam et al. [38] explored the contribution and application of mobile technologies in removing knowledge and information barriers for visually impaired visitors, while Ribeiro et al. [39] investigated the accessibility of mobile apps for tourists with disabilities to enhance their travel experiences. Altinay Özdemir [40] investigated the roles of virtual and augmented reality in tourism accessibility and marketing, finding that these technologies have both strengths and weaknesses with respect to tourism. While virtual reality offers a secure environment and alternative access, its disadvantages include user neglect and high user costs. Similarly, augmented reality can enrich knowledge and enhance experiences, but it comes with high costs and a lack of security. Therefore, the high costs of both technologies reduce their diffusion, creating a barrier to AT. Despite the fragmented nature of these scientific contributions, they highlight the relevance of smart technologies in upholding universal design values and creating AT for all [41]. More recently, studies have shown that the role of technology continues to be overlooked [4] and that accessibility has not been extensively analysed in relation to the cohesion between the digital and the physical dimension [7].

Despite the research on the benefits of digital technologies in specific areas of tourism, there has been no attempt to strengthen the applicability of digital technologies to allow greater accessibility in the context of tourism.

1.3 Methodology

To gain insights into the conceptual evolution of AT in the light of technological developments, a systematic review of the literature was conducted. This approach enabled a synthesis of the extant knowledge into a comprehensive framework and the identification of possible future research directions [42].

The literature review followed the four steps proposed by Denyer and Tranfield [42]: (a) formulation and definition of keywords; (b) definition of inclusion criteria; (c) selection and evaluation of materials; and (d) analysis and synthesis of the selected material.

A literature search was conducted using Scopus, one of the most authoritative and comprehensive databases of published scientific research [43]. The search was carried out in the 'title, author, keywords, abstract' field using the search string ('accessible tourism') AND (technolog* OR digital OR mobile OR web*), generating a total of 218 records. Only articles, books and book chapters were considered for analysis, while conference proceedings were excluded, leaving 163 records. Given that English is the accepted global language of research, articles in other languages were removed,

Fig. 1.1 Selection process

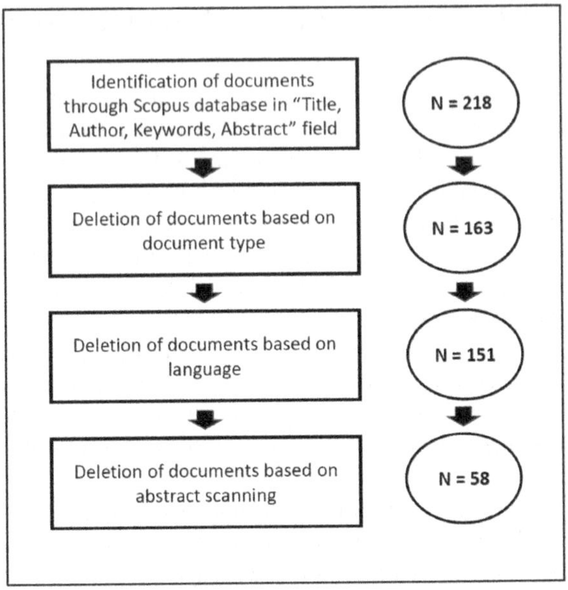

leaving 151 documents. These remaining documents were analysed in more detail, and their abstracts were scanned to ensure alignment with the objectives of the study. Documents not relevant to the purpose of the study were removed. Finally, 58 documents in total were included in the literature review. Figure 1.1 provides an overview of the selection process.

Using Excel, documents were categorised by year of publication, author, source of publication and document type. Next, to identify the tourist segments relevant to AT and the role of technology in AT, content analysis was conducted [44].

1.4 Results

This section presents both the descriptive results of the literature review and the results of the content analysis.

1.4.1 Descriptive Results

While the first studies on AT date back to the early 2000s [45], the first article on AT and technology was published in 2009 [46]. Since then, scholars have paid increasing attention to the topic, with a peak of 14 articles in 2020 and 11 in 2022, as reported in Fig. 1.2.

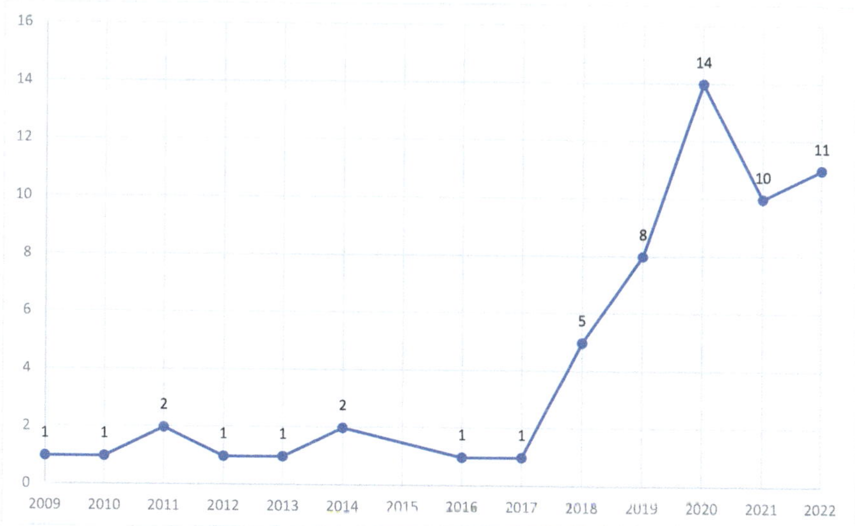

Fig. 1.2 Year of publication

The vast majority of documents on AT and technology were journal articles (n = 54; 93%), while the remaining were book chapters (n = 4; 7%). These data are reported in Fig. 1.3.

Fig. 1.3 Document type

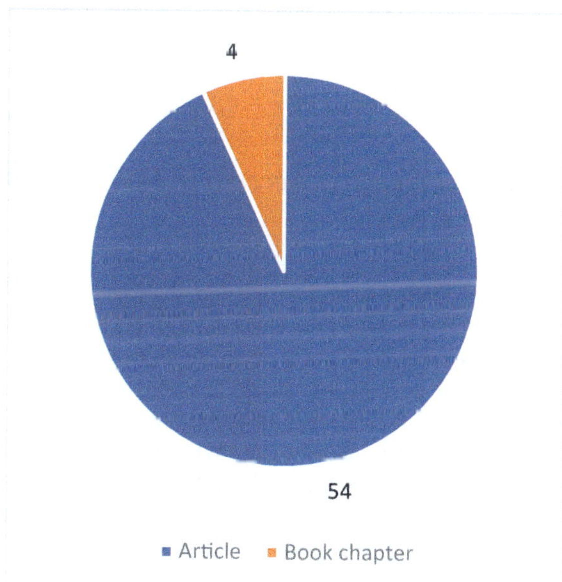

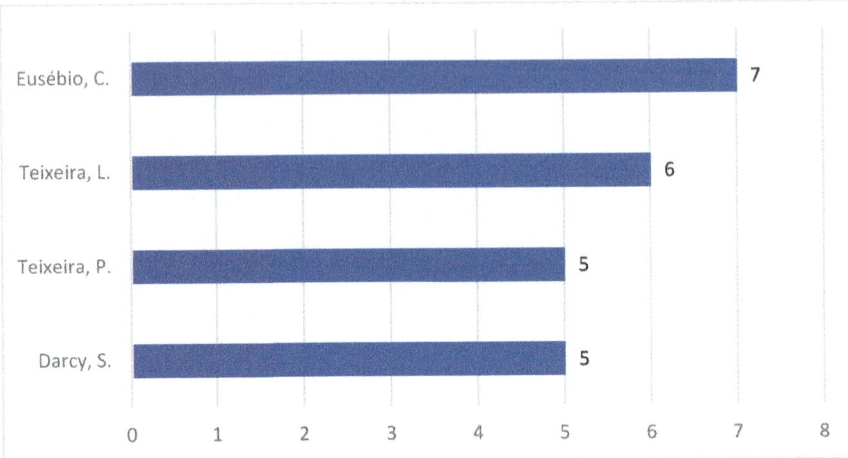

Fig. 1.4 Main authors. *Note* Authors with at least five publications

The most prolific authors investigating AT and technology were Celeste Eusébio (ten documents), Leonor Teixeira (six documents) and Pedro Teixeira (five documents) from the University of Aveiro, Portugal, and Simon Darcy from the University of Technology Sydney, Australia (five documents). These authors are reported in Fig. 1.4.

Journal articles on AT and technology were mostly published in *Sustainability Switzerland* (seven articles), *Journal of Accessibility and Design for All* (three articles) and *Current Issues in Tourism* (three articles). Main journals are reported in Fig. 1.5.

1.4.2 Segments in Accessible Tourism and Technology Research

To be fully inclusive and accessible, the tourism industry must consider the requirements of anyone with special needs [47]. Technological solutions can help to increase the accessibility of tourism products and services [37].

While AT pertains to various segments of the population with distinct needs and requirements [48], the results of the literature review show that the vast majority of the AT research is focused on PwD. According to the World Health Organization (https://www.who.int/topics/disabilities/en/), 15% of the world's population experiences some kind of disability. Therefore, this tourist segment represents an enormous business opportunity. While most studies have investigated general aspects of disability [e.g., 48, 49], some have focused on specific disabilities and impairments.

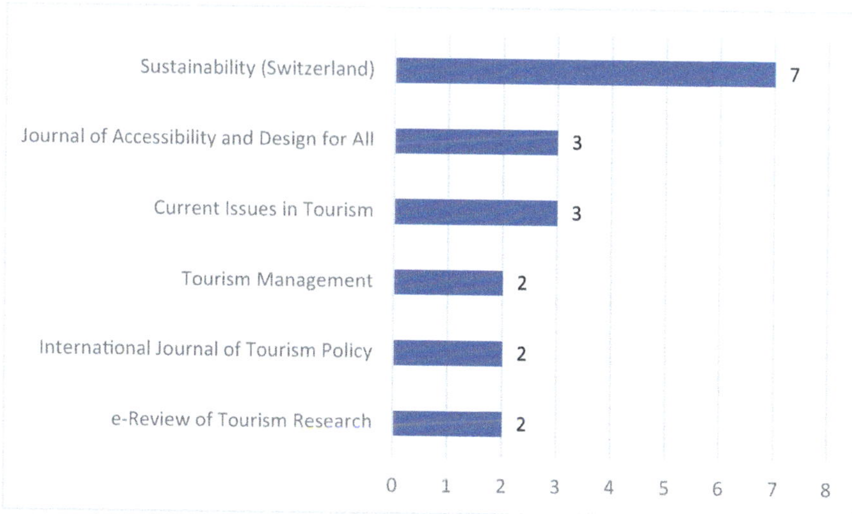

Fig. 1.5 Main journals. *Note* Journal with at least two publications

Physical and mobility disabilities [e.g., 50, 51] have been more frequently investigated compared with other types of disabilities, such as visual [e.g., 38] and hearing impairments [e.g., 52] and mental or cognitive disabilities [e.g., 53].

Few AT studies have focused temporary disabilities. Tourists with temporary disabilities are often regarded as having special access needs [e.g., 54] but have not been studied in detail because their disabilities are assimilable to permanent impairments. Similarly, the so-called invisible disabilities have rarely been investigated. Only one study [55] focused on the 'invisible' condition of epilepsy, shedding light on the main barriers faced by people with epilepsy when travelling, including the invisibility of the condition and the mechanisms used to cope with anxiety. In the article, the author stresses the importance of considering new and emerging technologies to support independent travel, as done with more common intellectual disabilities.

Senior tourists represent another important tourist segment in the AT and technology research. The ageing population is a macro-trend in contemporary society, and senior tourists have become an increasingly relevant segment for tourist service providers [56]. Senior tourists are considered a tourism segment with special needs because they may have accessibility requirements similar to those with mobility, sensory and mental impairments [57]. Darcy [35] revealed the nexus between the ageing population and disability. The literature highlights the issues of digital literacy [58] and accessibility to information and communication technologies (ICTs) [46] for elderly tourists, showing that as the age of tourists increase, their familiarity with ICTs and Internet use decreases.

Families with children represent another segment with special needs in the AT and technology research, albeit to a lesser extent. These studies highlight families with young children [54] and pregnant women [59] as segments with special access needs, but their specific requirements have not been investigated in detail.

Remarkably, the AT research has completely overlooked other tourist segments that have been traditionally excluded from tourism, including people with food intolerances, solo travellers, solo female travellers, LGBTIQ+ people and ethnic minorities. These topics did not appear in document titles, keywords or abstracts.

1.4.3 The Role of Digital Technologies in Accessible Tourism

This section presents the digital technologies associated with the AT research, namely ICTs and online information accessibility, mobile applications, virtual reality, Industry 4.0 and innovative and emerging technologies.

Most research on the role of digital technologies in AT has focused on the accessibility of ICTs. The absence of accessible information is one of the main barriers faced by people with special needs when they plan to travel [60]. Hence, this stream of research highlights the key role of technology in enhancing access to tourism products and services for people with special needs [61]. The accessibility of online information is a key topic in the research on PwD and AT because access to information prior to a trip is critical in decision-making by PwD [35, 62, 63]. Beneficiaries of online information accessibility also include people with specific or temporary disabilities [e.g., 50, 59] and elderly people [46]. In this respect, researchers have investigated the digital literacy of elderly tourists and their familiarity with the Internet, QR codes and NFC technology [58]. Families with children have been acknowledged as a segment with special requirements, but their information access needs have not been analysed in detail [54].

The literature on ICT accessibility has focused on different aspects. First, ICTs have been investigated at the destination or Destination Management Organization (DMO) level [e.g., 46]. These studies have mostly focused on the accessibility of official national tourism organisation websites in various countries around the world [63, 64] and the compliance of tourism-related websites with the Web Content Accessibility Guidelines 2.0 (WCAG 2.0) [e.g., 64]. Researchers have also investigated accessibility in relation to specific disabilities. Zajadacz [52] revealed that the Internet is primary source of information about tourist destinations for deaf people. Small et al. [65] highlighted the importance of information accessibility for people with visual impairments and understanding the multisensory nature of the overall tourist experience. With a specific focus on people with mobility disabilities, Altinay et al. [66] investigated the role of social media in sharing information about tourist destinations. Fernández-Díaz et al. [7] analysed DMO website accessibility for senior travellers and PwD. Other studies have investigated ICT accessibility at more specific levels, such as the accessibility of information about transportation systems for both PwD and senior tourists [56, 67]. Researchers have also investigated the accessibility of the hospitality sector in relation to PwD, with a focus on the websites of hotels [35, 62], OTAs [68, 69] and travel agencies [70]. Finally, some researchers have addressed the accessibility of information related to specific tourism products and attractions for people with both general and specific disabilities. For example, Mangani and Bassi [71] analysed the accessibility of Italian museum websites for PwD and their families, while Dinis et al. [72] explored the accessibility of music event websites and social media for people with visual and hearing impairments.

While access to online information and communication in the pre-travel phase is crucial for PwD and other groups with special needs [59, 71], researchers have called for greater attention to be paid to technology use before and during travel [53]. Specific technological devices can make tourism more accessible during a trip. In this regard, mobile applications are another technology associated with the AT research. The role of mobile applications in AT is mostly in reference to PwD and senior tourists as beneficiaries. Ribeiro et al. [39, 73] provide an overview of mobile applications that can make tourism more accessible. Mayordomo-Martínez et al. [51] developed a mobile application to enhance AT for people with a mobility disability. Huang and Lau [74] explored the role of gamification techniques for people with visual impairments, finding that they can enhance engagement, motivation and enjoyment with respect to the tourism experience. Similarly, Lam et al. [38] revealed that mobile applications can remove knowledge constraints for people with visual impairments. Mobile applications for senior travellers experiencing cognitive and visual decline have also been explored [57].

Virtual reality is another digital technology that can make tourism more accessible, not only before but also during travel. Virtual reality is the third technology associated with AT, but few studies have addressed the topic [75–77], with PwD being the only tourist segment considered. Marasco and Balbi [76] explored virtual reality in heritage tourism with a focus on travellers with mobility impairments. Similarly, Njerekai [77] explored the role of virtual reality in making tourism more accessible to people with physical impairments. In their bibliometric analysis, Henríquez et al. [75] call for greater attention to new technologies such as virtual reality in making tourism more accessible for PwD.

The fourth technology associated with AT is Industry 4.0. Only one study [78] has explored the role of Industry 4.0 technologies in facilitating access to tourism products and services for PwD.

Finally, some studies have addressed innovative and emerging technologies at a general level. Again, these studies have focused only on PwD. Piechotka et al. [79] investigated the general role of innovative technologies in enhancing accessibility to tourist infrastructure for PwD. Cassia et al. [4] focused on digital ecosystem logics in enabling access to tourism for PwD, with a specific focus on physical and mobility impairments. McIntosh (2020) highlighted the importance of considering new and emerging technologies to support independent travel for people with invisible disabilities. Tlili et al. [37] reviewed the existing technologies for PwD and call for greater attention to emerging technologies. Ali et al. [53] analysed the intersection between technology and AT with a specific focus on intellectual disabilities and call for more research on innovative travel-related technologies. Table 1.1 summarises the main research findings.

Table 1.1 Research findings on AT and technology

Technology	Segment	Main references
Topic 1		
Destination or DMO online accessibility	People with special needs (PwSN)	Buhalis and Michopoulou [48] Lestari et al. [59] Medarić et al. [80] Alves et al. [61] Agrawal et al. [47]
	People with disabilities (PwD)	Vila and Brea [46] Buhalis and Michopoulou [48] Michopoulou and Buhalis [81] Domínguez Vila et al. [64] Domínguez Vila et al. [63] Kołodziejczak [82] Lestari et al. [59] Cockburn-Wootten and McIntosh [54] Fernández-Díaz et al. [7] Casais and Castro [50] Rucci and Porto [83] Nigg and Peters [84] Alves et al. [61] Sisto et al. [32]
	Mobility impairments	Altinay et al. [66] Cockburn-Wootten and McIntosh [54] Fernández-Díaz et al. [7] Casais and Castro [50]
	Visual impairments	Small et al. [65] Cockburn-Wootten and McIntosh [54] Agrawal et al. [47]
	Hearing impairments	Zajadacz [52]
	Mental impairments	Fernández-Díaz et al. [7]
	Temporary disabilities	Vila and Brea [46] Lestari et al. [59] Cockburn-Wootten and McIntosh [54]
	Invisible disabilities	Cockburn-Wootten and McIntosh [54]

(continued)

Table 1.1 (continued)

Technology	Segment	Main references
	Seniors	Vila and Brea [46] Lestari et al. [59] Fernández-Díaz et al. [7] Cockburn-Wootten and McIntosh [54] Vieira et al. [58]
	Families with children	Lestari et al. [59] Cockburn-Wootten and McIntosh [54]
Transportation online accessibility	PwD	Ferreira et al. [67]
	Mobility impairments	Ferreira et al. [67] Rosa et al. [56]
	Seniors	Ferreira et al. [67] Rosa et al. [56]
Hospitality online accessibility	PwSN	Teixeira et al. [60]
	PwD	Wu et al. [85] Darcy [35] Darcy [62] Eusébio et al. [70] Singh and Sibi [68] Singh and Ismail [69] Teixeira et al. [86] Nigg and Peters [84]
Tourist attraction online accessibility	PwD	Mangani and Bassi [71] Henriques et al. [87]
	Visual impairments	Dinis et al. [72] Fryer [88]
	Hearing impairments	Dinis et al. [72]
Topic 2		
Mobile applications	PwD	Ribeiro et al. [73] Henríquez et al. [75]
	Mobility impairments	Mayordomo-Martínez et al. [51]
	Visual impairments	Huang and Lau [74] Lam et al. [38]
	Seniors	Bosch and Gharaveis [57]
Topic 3		
Virtual reality	PwD	Henríquez et al. [75]
	Mobility impairments	Marasco and Balbi [76] Njerekai [77]
Topic 4		
Industry 4.0	PwD	Teixeira et al. [78]
Topic 5		

(continued)

Table 1.1 (continued)

Technology	Segment	Main references
Need for innovative and emerging technologies	PwD	De La Fuente-Robles et al. [89] Piechotka et al. [79] Tlili et al. [37]
	Mobility impairments	Cassia et al. [4]
	Mental impairments	Ali et al. [53]
	Invisible disabilities	McIntosh [55]

1.5 Future Research Directions

The literature review shows that the concept of AT is still largely focused on the segment of people with physical and motor disabilities. However, the interdisciplinary nature of studies conducted across disciplines such as architecture and design may guarantee the application of universal design values and building AT for all. Nevertheless, there continues to be limited understanding of temporary and invisible disabilities. The latter are increasingly being linked to intellectual disabilities, which may particularly benefit from new digital technologies.

The results of the literature review renew the calls for research on technologies such as virtual reality and Industry 4.0, which have been largely overlooked in the literature. Additionally, the role of mobile applications should be investigated in more detail and with reference to specific disabilities or other segments with special access needs.

The gaps identified in the literature review suggest some specific research directions. Future AT studies should focus on:

- other segments to shed more light on specific disabilities, including intellectual and invisible disabilities, food intolerances, solo travellers, families with children, LGBTIQ+ people and ethnic minorities. These individuals have special needs but, despite being widespread in reality, have not been adequately studied in the literature.
- other technologies such as mobile applications for specific segments, virtual reality, Industry 4.0 and innovative technologies. Enabling accessibility to information before a journey is not enough—attention must also be paid to technologies that facilitate accessibility throughout the journey.

References

1. A. Bonfanti, G. Mion, F. Brunetti, A. Vargas-Sánchez, Bus. Strategy Environ. **1** (2022)
2. U. Gretzel, M. Sigala, Z. Xiang, C. Koo, Electron. Mark. **25**, 179 (2015)
3. D. Buhalis, Tour. Rev. **75**, 267 (2020)

4. F. Cassia, P. Castellani, C. Rossato, C. Baccarani, TQM J. **33**, 205 (2021)
5. D. Buhalis, Y. Sinarta, J. Travel Tour. Mark. **36**, 563 (2019)
6. Y. Zhang, S.T. Cole, Tour. Manag. **53**, 13 (2016)
7. E. Fernández-Díaz, C. Jambrino-Maldonado, P.P. Iglesias-Sánchez, C. de las Heras-Pedrosa, Tour. Rev. 1 (2022)
8. J. Im, Y.K. Chung, Tour. Manage. **95**, 104662 (2023)
9. T. Cox, *Cultural Diversity in Organizations: Theory, Research, and Practice* (Berrett-Koehler, San Francisco, 1993)
10. M.E. Mor-Barak, D.A. Cherin, Adm. Soc. Work **22**, 47 (1998)
11. R. Scheyvens, R. Biddulph, Tour. Geogr. **20**, 589 (2018)
12. A.H.Y. Hon, E. Gamor, Int. J. Tour. Res. **24**, 216 (2022)
13. S. Darcy, B. McKercher, S. Schweinsberg, Tour. Rev. **75**, 140 (2020)
14. D. Buhalis, S. Darcy, *Accessible Tourism: Concepts and Issues* (Channel View Publication, Bristol, 2011)
15. L. Nielsen, *Personas—User Focused Design* (Springer, London, 2013)
16. M. Zsarnoczky, L. David, Z. Mukayev, R. Baiburiev, GeoJ. Tour. Geosites. **22**, 224 (2016)
17. G. Waitt, K. Markwell, *Gay Tourism. Culture and Context* (Routledge, Florence, 2014)
18. Y. Ram, A. Kama, I. Mizrachi, C.M. Hall, J. Destin. Mark. Manag. **14**, 100374 (2019)
19. T.B. Vongvisitsin, A.K.F. Wong, Tour. Manage. **86**, 104331 (2021)
20. E.C.L. Yang, C. Khoo-Lattimore, C. Arcodia, Tour. Manage. **68**, 32 (2018)
21. M.S. Klemm, J. Travel Res. **41**, 85 (2002)
22. M. Battour, F. Hakimian, M. Ismail, E. Boğan, J. Islamic Market. **9**, 823 (2018)
23. J. Jafari, N. Scott, Ann. Tour. Res. **44**, 1 (2014)
24. S. Gopalan, U. Khalid, Tour. Recreation Res. 1 (2022)
25. S. McCabe, Ann. Tour. Res. **36**, 667 (2009)
26. S. McCabe, S. Johnson, Ann. Tour. Res. **41**, 42 (2013)
27. L. Minnaert, R. Maitland, G. Miller, Ann. Tour. Res. **36**, 316 (2009)
28. J. Zheng, S. Liang, J. Ma, G. Liu, Y. Wu, Ann. Tour. Res. **93**, 103372 (2022)
29. B. Gillovic, A. McIntosh, Sustainability **12**, 9722 (2020)
30. J.L. Crompton, Ann. Tour. Res. **6**, 408 (1979)
31. T. Bornhorst, J.B. Ritchie, L. Sheehan, Tour. Manage. **31**, 572 (2010)
32. R. Sisto, G.M. Cappelletti, P. Bianchi, E. Sica, Curr. Issue Tour. **25**, 8 (2022)
33. G. Ozogul, G. Güçlütürk Baran, J. Tour. Futures **2**, 79 (2016)
34. G. Qiao, L. Ding, L. Zhang, H. Yan, Tour. Rev. **77**, 713 (2021)
35. S. Darcy, Tour. Manage. **31**, 6 (2010)
36. International Organization for Standardization, *International Standard 21902. Tourism and Related Services—Accessible Tourism for All—Requirements and Recommendations* (ISO, Geneva, 2021)
37. A. Tlili, F. Altinay, Z. Altinay, Y. Zhang, Int. J. Contemp. Hosp. Manag. **33**, 4460 (2021)
38. K.L. Lam, C.S. Chan, M. Peters, J. Destin. Mark. Manag. **17**, 100434 (2020)
39. F.R. Ribeiro, A. Silva, F. Barbosa, A.P. Silva, J.C. Metrôlho, Inf. Technol. Tour. **19**, 29 (2018)
40. M. Altinay Özdemir, ICT tools and applications for accessible tourism, in *Advances in Hospitality, Tourism, and the Service Industry*, ed. by C. Eusébio, L. Teixeira, M. J. Carneiro (IGI Global Publisher, Hershey PA, 2021), p. 277
41. K.J. Lin, H. Ye, R. Law, J. Smart Tour. **2**, 5 (2022)
42. D. Denyer, D. Tranfield, *The Sage Handbook of Organizational Research Methods* (SAGE Publications, London, 2009)
43. P. Jacsó, Online Inf. Rev. **35**, 3 (2011)
44. S. Stemler, Practical assessment. Res. Eval. **7**, 17 (2001)
45. L. Sen, S. Mayfield, Public Works Manag. Policy **8**, 4 (2004)
46. T. Vila, J.A.F. Brea, Revista Galega de Economia **18**, 1 (2009)
47. G. Agrawal, A. Dumka, M. Singh, A. Bijalwan, J. Sens. **2022** (2022)
48. D. Buhalis, E. Michopoulou, Curr. Issue Tour. **14**, 2 (2011)
49. P. Bianchi, G.M. Cappelletti, E. Mafrolla, E., Sica, R. Sisto, R., Sustainability **12**, 23 (2020)

50. B. Casais, C. Castro, J. Hospitality Tour. Technol. **12**, 2 (2021)
51. D. Mayordomo-Martínez, J.C. Sánchez-Aarnoutse, J.M. Carrillo-de-Gea, J.A. García-Berná, J.L. Fernández-Alemán, G. García-Mateos, Int. J. Environ. Res. Public Health **16**, 12 (2019)
52. A. Zajadacz, Curr. Issue Tour. **17**, 5 (2014)
53. F. Ali, L. Cain, T.S. Legendre, L. Wu, J. Hospitality Tour. Res. **1**, 15 (2022)
54. C. Cockburn-Wootten, A. McIntosh, Sustainability **12**, 24 (2020)
55. A. McIntosh, Ann. Tour. Res. **81**, 102856 (2020)
56. M.P. Rosa, P. Pinto, H. Assunção, Int. J. Sustain. Dev. Plan. **15**, 6 (2020)
57. S.J. Bosch, A. Gharaveis, Appl. Ergon. **58**, 1 (2017)
58. G. Vieira, C. Manita, C., Ribeiro, M. P. Rosa, J. Accessibility Design All **12**, 2 (2022)
59. N.S. Lestari, R.D. Wiastuti, I. Triana, African Journal of Hospitality. Tourism and Leisure **8**, 4 (2019)
60. P. Teixeira, C. Eusébio, L. Teixeira, Tour. Hosp. Res. **22**, 2 (2022)
61. J. Alves, P. Teixeira, C. Eusébio, L. Teixeira, Appl. Sci. **12**, 8 (2022)
62. S. Darcy, Tour. Recreat. Res. **36**, 2 (2011)
63. T. Domínguez Vila, E. Alén González, S. Darcy, Scand. J. Hospitality Tour. **19**, 2 (2019)
64. T. Domínguez Vila, E. Alén González, S. Darcy, Disabil. Rehabil. **40**, 24 (2018)
65. J. Small, S. Darcy, T. Packer, Tour. Manage. **33**, 4 (2012)
66. Z. Altinay, T. Saner, N.M. Bahçelerli, F. Altinay, J. Educ. Technol. Soc. **19**, 1 (2016)
67. A. F. Ferreira, Y. Akasaka, M. Greiner de Oliveira Pinheiro, S. J. Chang, Sustainability **12**, 23 (2020)
68. R. Singh, P.S. Sibi, E-Rev. Tour. Res. **18**, 5 (2021)
69. R. Singh, A. Ismail, Appl. Ubiquitous Comput. **13**, 35 (2021)
70. C. Eusébio, A. Silveiro, L. Teixeira, J. Accessibility Des. All **10**, 2 (2020)
71. A. Mangani, L. Bassi, Int. J. Tour. Policy **9**, 4 (2019)
72. M.G. Dinis, C. Eusébio, Z. Breda, Int J. Event Festiv. Manag. **11**, 1 (2020)
73. F.R. Ribeiro, A. Silva, J.C. Metrôlho, A.P. Silva, F.S. Barbosa, Int. J. Mob. Comput. Multimedia Commun. (IJMCMC) **9**, 2 (2018)
74. L. Huang, N. Lau, Sustainability **12**, 15 (2020)
75. C.S. Henríquez, A.J.R. Cano, J.H. Galán, Y.M. de la Fuente-Robles, J. Accessibility Design All **12**, 1 (2022)
76. A. Marasco, B. Balbi, E-Rev. Tour. Res. **17**, 3 (2019)
77. C. Njerekai, J. Herit. Tour. **15**, 5 (2020)
78. P. Teixeira, L. Teixeira, C. Eusébio, *Handbook of Research on Social Media Applications for the Tourism and Hospitality Sector* (IGI Global, Hershey PA, 2019)
79. A.P. Piechotka, N. Lukasik, A.O. Tryzno, M. Piechotka, K. Sawicka, *Destination Management and Marketing: Breakthroughs in Research and Practice* (IGI Global, Hershey PA, 2020)
80. Z. Medarić, J. Sulyok, S. Kardos, J. Gabruč, Hung. Geog. Bull. **70**, 3 (2021)
81. E. Michopoulou, D. Buhalis, Inf. Manag. **50**, 5 (2013)
82. A. Kołodziejczak, Quaestiones Geographicae **38**, 2 (2019)
83. A.C. Rucci, N. Porto, Eur. J. Tour. Res. **31**, 1 (2022)
84. J.J. Nigg, M. Peters, J. Hosp. Tour. Manag. **52**, 1 (2022)
85. Y.C.J. Wu, C.L. Chang, Y.J. Hsieh, J. Univ. Comput. Sci. **20**, 15 (2014)
86. P. Teixeira, C. Eusébio, L. Teixeira, Int. J. Tour. Policy **11**, 3 (2021)
87. M.H. Henriques, M.L. Canales, A. García-Frank, M. Gomez-Heras, M. Geoheritage **11** (2019)
88. L. Fryer, Univ. Access Inf. Soc. **20**, 4 (2021)
89. Y.M. De La Fuente-Robles, M.D. Muñoz-de-Dios, A.B. Mudarra-Fernández, A.J. Ricoy-Cano, Sustainability **12**, 24 (2020)

Chapter 2
Accessible Tourism: The Demand-Side Perspective

Vania Vigolo and Francesca Simeoni

Abstract Accessibility is beneficial for anyone facing challenges in experiencing tourism, not only for people with disabilities. Therefore, the demand for accessible tourism is highly diverse and warrants in-depth analysis. Based on a systematic review of the scientific literature published since 2010, this chapter investigates the aspects characterizing the demand for accessible tourism. The analysis led to the identification of five major themes: market dimension and value, tourist experiences, travel motivations, travel constraints, and travel needs. Practical implications are derived for destination management organizations and tourism companies wishing to improve the accessibility of their offerings.

Keywords Accessible tourism demand · Tourists with disabilities · Tourist experiences · Travel motivations · Travel constraints · Travel needs

2.1 Introduction

Given the most recent and comprehensive conceptualizations and definitions of accessible tourism [1, 2], it is safe to say that not only people with disabilities but society as a whole can benefit from the economic, political, and social effects of accessibility [3]. The expanded definitions of disability [4] have led scholars to consider not only people with disabilities but anyone experiencing difficulties accessing or enjoying tourism, such as senior travelers, the beneficiaries of accessible tourism [5, 6]. According to the World Health Organization, these difficulties may result from a reduction in capacity, whether physical, sensory, intellectual, or emotional [7]. Given this range of impairments, the beneficiaries of accessible tourism cannot be considered a single market segment. Indeed, according to the World Tourism Organization (WTO), "accessible tourism refers to continuing efforts to ensure that all people have

V. Vigolo (✉) · F. Simeoni
University of Verona, Verona, Italy
e-mail: vania.vigolo@univr.it

F. Cassia et al. (eds.), *Accessible Tourism in the Digital Ecosystem*,
SpringerBriefs in Applied Sciences and Technology,
https://doi.org/10.1007/978-3-031-38782-1_2

access to tourism destinations, products, and services, regardless of their physical limitations, disability or age" [2].

The characteristics and needs of people with special needs, such as those with hearing or visual impairments [8], learning difficulties, mobility issues or dependent on wheelchairs, age-related issues (e.g., elderly people or children), or a particularly small or large stature, differ greatly. Moreover, only 9% of tourism providers in the European Union (EU) promote themselves as "accessible" [9], even if, in reality, this is not backed up by the services they provide [10]. Approximately 18% of all inhabitants in the EU are demanding accessible tourism, and it has been estimated that this rate may increase if operators respond to emerging service requests.

Accessible tourism should not be considered "special" [11] but rather as tourism services that offer accessibility in terms of accommodation, transport, information, general facilities, and emerging technologies to meet accessible hospitality and tourism needs [12].

While some literature reviews on accessible tourism have previously been published [2, 13], they address a variety of perspectives without focusing specifically on the accessible tourism market and its characteristics. This chapter aims to contribute to the knowledge on the accessible tourism market by systematically investigating and synthesizing the existing literature on tourist characteristics and travel behaviors.

The remainder of this chapter is organized as follows. Section 2.2 overviews trends in the accessible tourism market. Section 2.3 explains the methods adopted for the systematic literature review. Section 2.4 presents the descriptive and thematic findings. Finally, Sect. 2.5 discusses the results, limitations, and future research directions are provided.

2.2 The Accessible Tourist Market: An Overview

In recent years, governments and public institutions have drawn attention to accessible tourism, both to meet human rights and as a potential business opportunity for tourism destinations. Estimations with respect to the size and potential value of the accessible travel market are inconsistent across countries and regions. The WTO [6], one of the most authoritative sources of accessible tourism information, reports that about 15% of the world's population lives with some form of disability and thus may require accessible tourism facilities and services. Along with the social benefits of accessible tourism, the economic benefits for the tourism industry are significant given the size of the accessible tourism market. The European Network for Accessible Tourism estimates that the accessible tourism market is worth €500 billion per year in Europe alone.

According to the WTO [6], the potential tourist market segment of people with disabilities in the EU comprises more than 80 million people (or 130 million people when including their travel companions). In fact, tourists with access requirements travel with an average of 1.5 companions, stay at tourist destinations for longer periods, make more repeat visits, and travel throughout the year, reducing the seasonality of certain destinations, thus generating more revenue on average compared with conventional tourists [14]. The international dimension appears to be particularly affected by tourists with accessibility needs, with an estimated 75% more international tourists when accessibility is improved.

Of particular relevance is the senior segment [15], which represents 65% of the accessible tourism market segment. This segment has particular characteristics, including the number of trips per year (six to seven), the highest discretionary income, and an increased tendency to travel overseas [16]. Therefore, the accessibility of destinations, tourism facilities, attractions, and services has become an urgent issue for destination management organizations (DMOs) and the tourism industry in general.

2.3 Methods

This chapter is based on a systematic literature review, providing an overview of studies on accessible tourism from the demand-side perspective. Systematic literature reviews involve several steps [17]: (i) formulation of a research question to focus the literature review; (ii) identification of documents for review; (iii) article selection and evaluation; and (iv) analysis and synthesis of the main themes that emerge from the literature. The research question this review intends to answer is the following: *what are the main themes that have been investigated in the literature regarding accessible tourism from a demand-side perspective?* In line with Yung and Khoo-Lattimore [18], the Scopus database was used to locate studies. To identify relevant articles, the search term "accessible touris*" was used in the "article title, abstract, and keywords" fields. Articles were limited to the fields of business, management, and accounting, and document type was limited to research articles and reviews written in English. As suggested by Agapito [19], only journal articles were selected because they are considered the best representation of knowledge on tourism. No chronological restrictions were employed. Overall, Scopus returned 114 documents, which were further evaluated. Following abstract screening, studies that did not focus on the demand side of accessible tourism were excluded, reducing the sample to 55 articles. Once the full text of each article had been read, 13 articles were excluded because they were not relevant to this research. Thus, the final sample comprised 42 papers.

2.4 Findings

This section presents descriptive analyses of the 42 articles selected and reviewed. The analyses include the distribution of publications over time and across journals and authors, the geographical focus of the research, research methodologies, and main keywords. Researchers have explored accessible tourism from the demand perspective only in the last decade, with the first two papers on accessible tourism being published in 2010 [20, 21]. From 2010 to 2017, the publication of papers was relatively consistent before increasing in 2017 and peaking in 2022, when 11 articles were published (26% of the selected papers) (see Fig. 2.1).

The distribution of publications across journals is varied, with 29 leading journals publishing articles on accessible tourism from a demand-side perspective. Of these, 20 journals (69%) have published only one article, and six (21%) have published two articles. *Tourism Review* and *Tourism Recreation Research* each have three publications, while the leading journal is *Current Issues in Tourism* with four publications.

Among the selected papers, four were published in journals given a ranking of 4* by the Academic Journal Guide (AJG): *Tourism Management* (two articles), *Annals of Tourism Research* (one article), and *Journal of Travel Research* (one article). Two articles were published in journals ranked AJG 3: *Information & Management* and the *Journal of Sustainable Tourism*. The remaining articles were published in journals ranked AJG 2 or AJG 1.

Three authors have predominantly published on this topic over the years: Simon Darcy (five articles), Celeste Eusébio (four articles), and Elizabeth Kastenholz (three articles).

The predominant countries considered in studies on tourists with disabilities were Australia (seven articles), Portugal (six articles), and Italy (five articles), followed by Spain and the UK, with four works each.

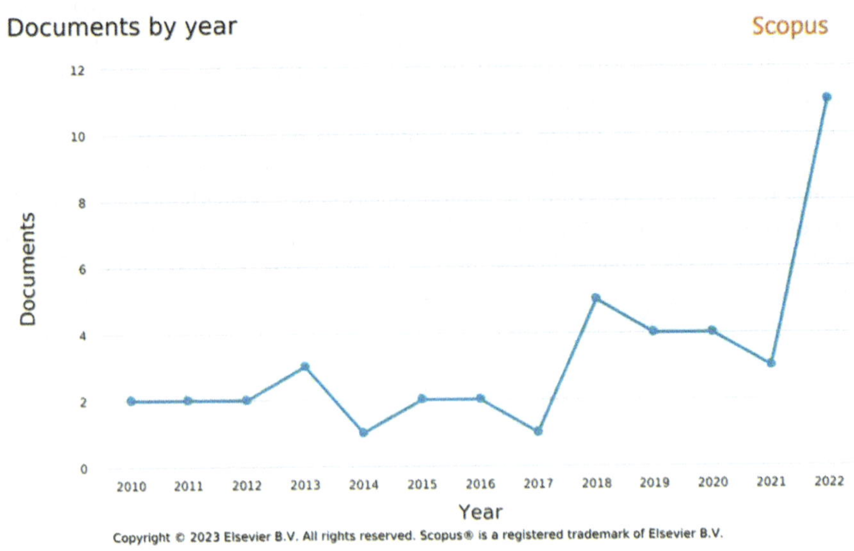

Fig. 2.1 Number of selected papers by year

Fig. 2.2 Main keywords found in selected articles

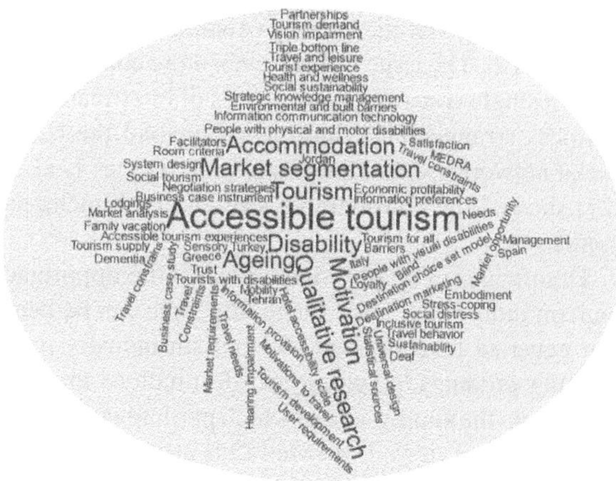

The selected publications are mainly based on qualitative research methods (23 studies), followed by quantitative methods (15 studies), mixed methods (three articles), and reviews (one article). Only 11 articles presented case studies.

The most common keywords used were *accessible tourism* (16 times) and *disability* (14 times) (see Fig. 2.2). Of the different types of disabilities, aging was the only keyword mentioned more than once. The main subthemes in the studies were motivation, accommodation issues, and market segmentation. However, the most important aspect that emerged is the multitude and variety of selected keywords, highlighting the complexity of the phenomenon and the fact that, at least in terms of the scientific literature, we have not yet developed a sufficient framework of the most critical issues.

2.4.1 *Emerging Themes from the Analysis*

From the analysis of the papers selected for this study, five major recurring themes emerged, corresponding to five categories of papers: the dimensions and importance of the accessible tourism market, the importance of the tourist experience, travel motivations, travel constraints, and travel needs.

2.4.1.1 The Dimensions and Importance of the Accessible Tourism Market

Social developments have transformed tourism from being merely desirable to being a necessity [22], even a primary social need [13], for tourists both with and without disabilities. Tourism is a socioeconomic phenomenon and is highly influenced by social inequality.

However, given the limited existing data, measuring accessible tourism is challenging [13]. The issue is made even more complex by the fact that accessible tourism is not a single construct but "a series of interrelated, overlapping, and interdependent business arrangements that extend beyond the business entity through a series of social networks within the destination region" [21]. Using a case study, Darcy et al. [21] showed the considerable size and multiniche nature of the accessible tourism market.

Domínguez et al. [23] demonstrated the importance of accessible tourism for the tourism industry. A wide range of people can be beneficiaries of accessible tourism and generate revenue, and the tourism industry must recognize the importance of defining products, services, and destinations that are accessible to all. Based on a study from the supply side in which participants from major travel and leisure companies were interviewed, Bowtell [24] arrived at the same conclusion. The accessible tourism market is viewed as a distinct sector with significant growth prospects, with an estimated projection of €88.6 billion by 2025 in potential revenue. Tourists with disabilities spend 1.16 times more than those without disabilities. Nevertheless, to date, few travel and leisure companies strive to satisfy the need for accessible tourism by offering accessible products and services.

2.4.1.2 Importance of the Tourist Experience

Previous researchers have aimed to identify whether the tourism experience is important for people with disabilities. Rubio-Escuderos et al. [4] conducted in-depth interviews with 25 people with reduced mobility, finding that their tourism experiences had a decisive impact on their perceptions of their disabilities in daily life, in particular their sense of independence. Similarly, Gillovic et al. [25] interviewed nine adults with intellectual disabilities, all of whom reported that their tourist experiences facilitated positive outcomes in terms of their interpersonal relationships, social interactions, and inclusion. Through their travel experiences, many of the participants "achieved personal goals, cultivated growing passions, uncovered new interests and tried new things" [25], boosting their sense of self-efficacy, competence, and self-confidence. The participants also expressed that the tourist experience gave them a sense of normality that they are typically denied in their daily lives. In fact, as Chung and Lee [26] point out, tourism is the least frequent recreational activity for people with disabilities.

The findings of studies on the importance of the tourist experience for people with disabilities suggest that there are significant motivations for the tourism industry to invest in accessible tourist experiences. Analyses of the behaviors of tourists with disabilities may help in understanding the aspects in which to invest. For instance, exploring the types of people with whom tourists with disabilities choose to travel, the criteria on which they base this decision, and their level of satisfaction when actually traveling with them would be of interest. Chung and Lee [26] found a significant gap between desired companions and those that people with disabilities actually travel with, affecting the frequency of tourism experiences. People with disabilities often have "more difficulty finding the right companions, the right time, and the right places for travel than people without disabilities" [26]. It would be of interest to expand on the factors identified by Rubio Escuderos et al. influencing the decision to travel, including the "limited negotiating scope, necessity of a care assistant, knowledge of the destination language or availability of state aid" [4]. Moreover, traveling companions play an important role in transportation between destinations, with train services potentially being the most convenient form of transport if stations are well-organized.

Finally, travel-related technologies are an important determinant of or deterrent to tourism and may help address problems related to different disabilities during travel. According to Ali et al. [27], these technologies must meet certain standards with respect to user-friendliness, comprehensibility, usefulness, and reliability. The authors also identified the individual, social, and situational factors influencing disabled tourists' experiences of technology.

The study of travel behaviors also depends on the type of trip and destination. For example, Rahmafitria et al. [28] found three dimensions affecting the accessibility of protected islands: destination accessibility, individual accessibility, and protected island accessibility. What unites all of these studies is that the perception of difficult accessibility influences tourists' decisions to visit the destination.

In conclusion, as also claimed by the authors cited, more research on the experiences and behaviors of tourists with disabilities is needed, and many aspects still remain to be confirmed or refuted.

2.4.1.3 Travel Motivations

Motivations to travel arise from the expected benefits of the tourist experience [29], including pleasure, increased knowledge, well-being, and personal development. In a mixed methodology study involving semi-structured interviews and questionnaires administered to 348 respondents, Moura et al. [29] highlighted the differences in motivations between people with disabilities who had had previous tourism experiences and those who had not. Those with previous tourist experiences perceived fewer benefits compared with those without previous experiences. It would be of interest to explore the reasons for previous experiences resulting in a subsequent lower motivation to travel and to address these influencing factors.

Gassiot Melian et al. [30] investigated accessible tourism at religious sites, showing that the perceived value of accessibility may be a determinant of satisfaction and loyalty and that the weight of these values is different for people with and without disabilities. Of the two groups, tourists with special needs were influenced more by the perceived value of accessibility, consequently influencing their motivation to travel again.

To increase the motivation to travel, information and communication technologies that offer a wide range of possibilities to improve accessibility to tourist services should be developed [31]. To date, it appears that the greatest barrier to implementing these systems is the weak standardization of existing websites, mobile applications, booking platforms, and social media. Nigg and Peters [31] found that all stakeholders, including people with disabilities and their organizations, hospitality and tourism service providers, and government agencies, agree with this conclusion.

Moura et al. [32] found that another important travel motivation for people with disabilities is the increased ability to cope with stress. From the results of their empirical study on 306 respondents, the authors concluded that tourism for people with disabilities may even be therapeutic, with the increase in personal and social resources during travel positively contributing to their health and well-being. Given these results, the authors encourage the development of new tourism products and policies.

2.4.1.4 Travel Constraints

Several papers on accessible tourism have investigated the barriers or constraints to travel intentions, including travelers' intrinsic constraints (e.g., [33]). For example, using a mixed-methods' approach, Qiao et al. [8] explored the physiological and psychological barriers to travel for people with vision impairments, finding that internal psychological perceptions, perceived behavioral control, and perceived social intentions positively affect their travel intentions. Other studies have focused on extrinsic constraints related to destinations or tourism services. For example, Mahmoudzadeh and Sarjaz [34] investigated environmental barriers in Tehran for people with physical and motor disabilities. The three major barriers that emerged from the findings were related to transportation, attractions, and accommodation.

In a recent quantitative study, De Pascale et al. [35] explored the influence of gender on the motivation to travel for people with disabilities, finding that women with disabilities were more affected by "personal skills, absence of a travel partner, availability of suitable accommodation, transport difficulties and, partially, by the ability to plan a vacation" compared with men with disabilities.

Several studies on accessible tourism have specifically focused on older tourists, a growing segment of the tourism market [36]. In this regard, Wan et al. [37] adopted a qualitative method to examine the accessibility of heritage sites for older tourists. The major barriers identified in interviews with participants included feeling unsafe and crowded, the effort required to use facilities, unclear and insufficient signage, and cluttered public lavatories. Gregory [38] adopted an autoethnographic study to explore adventure travel (i.e., diving experiences) for older women, while Eddy-U et al. [39] explored accessibility barriers for seniors visiting large-scale tourism facilities such as integrated resorts. The findings of these studies show that older people face environmental barriers related to integrated resort design.

Scholars have also examined the role of technology in reducing travel barriers in terms of improved access to information and destinations. For example, Teixeira et al. [40] explored the accessibility of Portuguese hotel websites, finding that a lack or low level of website accessibility reduces travel intentions, thus reducing travel possibilities for people with disabilities. In addition, Lam et al. [41] highlighted the role of technology in removing knowledge barriers regarding urban destinations for visually impaired tourists. To overcome travel barriers, people with visual disabilities rely on negotiation strategies, which can be categorized into personal, travel organization, and interpersonal strategies [42].

While research on accessible tourism has traditionally focused on people with physical and motor disabilities, recent attention has been paid to travel barriers faced by people with invisible conditions. For example, McIntosh [43] investigated the travel experiences of people with epilepsy, identifying three main challenges: seizure episodes, the invisibility of the condition, and the management of anxiety. Similarly, using a quantitative study, Freund et al. [44] examined the travel constraints of families with children diagnosed with autism spectrum disorder, finding that travel intentions were influenced by the severity of the disorder and intrinsic travel constraints related to the individual's psychological condition, including "personality factors, attitudes, religious beliefs, and moods" (p. 608). Similarly, Nyman et al. [45] explored the travel constraints of families with wheelchair-bound children with cerebral palsy. The major barriers to travel for these tourists were inaccessible transport and accommodation facilities.

This overview of the literature highlights that a range of travel constraints may lead to lower travel intentions for people with special needs. While physiological and psychological conditions undoubtedly make travel more challenging for people with special needs, much can be done by public institutions and managers in the tourism industry to reduce external barriers and improve the accessibility of destinations and tourism services. An understanding of tourist needs, discussed in the next section, is the first step toward developing effective accessible tourism strategies.

2.4.1.5 Travel Needs

This section presents the research on tourists' diverse accessibility needs, which depend on tourism services and the type and severity of disability. Focusing on people with traditionally recognized types of disability (intellectual, motor, hearing, and visual) in Portugal, Figueiredo et al. [46] explored various aspects of travel behavior, including travel motivations and attitudes, the relevance of destination features, and preferred recreational activities at the destination. The differences that emerged between people with different disabilities imply the existence of diverse accessibility needs depending on the disability.

Some scholars have investigated the role of technology in responding to tourists' accessibility needs, viewing technology as a means of improving the overall inclusiveness of the tourist experience. For example, Buhalis and Michopoulou [47] analyzed the role of information and communication technologies as an enabler of tourist needs. Similarly, Marasco and Balbi [48] qualitatively explored the needs of visitors with mobility impairments at heritage sites to improve the design of virtual reality experiences.

Other studies have focused on tourists' information needs. For example, Michopoulou and Buhalis [49] explored the information needs of people with disabilities and the technical difficulties that can emerge when addressing these needs. Interestingly, the authors highlight the need to personalize travel information searches and media according to tourists' special needs. Further, Zajadacz [50] used a quantitative survey to understand the information needs of Deaf people. The results show that along with word of mouth from friends and family, the Internet is one of the main sources of tourist information for both hearing and deaf people. Zajadacz [50] highlights that compared with hearing people, a smaller percentage of deaf people use the Internet as a source of information.

Naniopoulos et al. [51] used a qualitative method to understand tourists' needs and promote accessible tourism in Turkey and Greece. Specifically, the authors considered both the needs of both tourists with disabilities and people who face difficulties in their daily activities "as a consequence of the inadequacies of their environment" (p. 60), such as pregnant women, young children, and older individuals. Accessibility needs were examined in relation to accommodation, tourism support facilities, cultural sites, transportation, and open spaces in urban and natural environments.

Based on a qualitative study, Small et al. [52] investigated the tourist experience of tourists with visual impairments, identifying a major theme in the need for inclusion in terms of access to information, wayfinding, and traveling with a guide dog.

Some studies have concentrated on analyzing specific services within the tourism industry such as hospitality services. For example, Darcy [20] focused on accessible accommodation, specifically the importance of hotel room selection criteria. In a later study, Darcy [53] integrated consumer, business, and government perspectives on accessible tourism and presented a framework for individual accessible accommodation information provision.

2.5 Discussion and Implications

Based on a systematic analysis of studies on accessible tourism published since 2010, this paper identified some major themes regarding accessible tourism from a demand-side perspective and contributes to the knowledge on the market characteristics in terms of its dimensions, the importance of the tourist experience, travel motivations, travel constraints, and travel needs. Several managerial implications issues can be derived from the results.

First, tourists with disabilities represent a heterogeneous market; thus, there is a need to improve segmentation criteria to design and implement successful tourism management and marketing strategies. While the type and severity of disability may be useful for identifying some tourist segments, DMOs and the tourism industry should consider other criteria to identify specific tourist profiles.

Second, given the heterogeneity that characterizes the accessible tourism market, it is essential to understand how tourists differ in terms of their perceived importance of the travel experience, motivations, constraints, and travel needs. DMOs and tourism companies should invest in market research to improve their knowledge of the market and understand the importance of applying a multi-segmented marketing approach and personalization of services.

Third, designing accessible tourism experiences is paramount for attracting tourists with special needs, be they people with disabilities, older individuals, or individuals with specific permanent or temporary accessibility needs. Offering accessible tourism experiences can help improve destinations and firms' competitiveness in this market while simultaneously improving the quality of experience for tourists in general. Technology represents a valuable tool for enhancing the accessibility of destinations and tourist offerings during various phases of the tourism process, including the identification of tourists needs, the provision of accessible and updated information, the offerings of travel organizations, and the actual tourist experience at the destination. In addition, infrastructural and structural investments are required at both the destination and the firm levels to reduce or potentially eliminate physical barriers to public transport, accommodation, and tourist attractions. DMOs and policymakers may also play an important role in training and educating professionals about the range of needs for different market segments. By working together, DMOs, policymakers, and the tourism industry can promote accessible tourism, enhance the visitor experience for tourists with disabilities, and contribute to the overall growth of the tourism industry.

References

1. S. Darcy, B. McKercher, S. Schweinsberg, From tourism and disability to accessible tourism: a perspective article. Tour. Rev. **75**, 140 (2020). https://doi.org/10.1108/TR-07-2019-0323
2. G. Qiao, L. Ding, L. Zhang, H. Yan, Accessible tourism: a bibliometric review (2008–2020). Tour. Rev. **77**, 713 (2021). https://doi.org/10.1108/TR-12-2020-0619
3. J.A.C. Soler, M.B. Díaz, P.S. Vera, El turismo social accesible como nuevo modelo turístico [Accessible social tourism as a new tourist model], Cuadernos de Turismo **41**, 139 (2018). https://doi.org/10.6018/turismo.41.326981
4. L. Rubio-Escuderos, H. García-Andreu, E. Michopoulou, D. Buhalis, Perspectives on experiences of tourists with disabilities: implications for their daily lives and for the tourist industry. Tour. Recreat Res. **10**(1080/02508281), 1981071 (2021)
5. S. Darcy, T.J. Dickson, A whole-of-life approach to tourism: the case for accessible tourism experiences. J. Hosp. Tour. Manag. **16**, 32 (2009). https://doi.org/10.1375/jhtm.16.1.32
6. World Tourism Organization, *Manual on Accessible Tourism for All: Principles, Tools and Best Practices—Module I: Accessible Tourism—Definition and Context* (UNWTO, 2016). https://doi.org/10.18111/9789284418077
7. D. Popović, I. Slivar, M. Gonan Božac, Accessible tourism and formal planning: current state of Istria County in Croatia, Adm. Sci. **12**, 181 (2022). https://doi.org/10.3390/admsci12040181
8. G. Qiao, Y. Cao, J. Zhang, Accessible tourism—understanding blind and vision-impaired tourists' behaviour towards inclusion. Tour. Rev. https://doi.org/10.1108/tr-03-2022-0129
9. V. Eichhorn, Economic impact and travel patterns of accessible tourism in Europe—final report (European Commission, Director-General Enterprise and Industry, 2014). https://ec.europa.eu/docsroom/documents/5566/attachments/1/translations/en/renditions/native

10. G. Sakalauskaitė, D. Šaparnienė, I. Reinholde, Accessible tourism development in the post-Soviet country context: a case of Klaipėda City, Lithuania. Sci. Pap. Univ. Pardubice Series D Fac. Econ. Adm. **28**, 126 (2020)
11. World Tourism Organization, Highlights of the 1st UNWTO Conference on Accessible Tourism in Europe (San Marino, 19–20 November 2014) (UNTWO, 2016). https://doi.org/10.18111/9789284417902
12. A. Tlili, F. Altinay, Z. Altinay, Y. Zhang, Envisioning the future of technology integration for accessible hospitality and tourism. Int. J. Contemp. Hosp. Manag. **33**, 4460 (2021). https://doi.org/10.1108/ijchm-03-2021-0321
13. A. Giusti, A. Viviani, Social diversity: a look at tourism. J. Environ. Manag. Tour. **4**, 57 (2013). www.journals.aserspublishing.eu/jemt/article/view/389
14. World Tourism Organization, *Manual on Accessible Tourism for All: Public–Private Partnerships and Good Practices* (UNWTO, 2015). https://doi.org/10.18111/9789284416585
15. D. Damiasih, A. Palestho, A.A.G. Raka, H. Kurniawan, P. Pebriani, S. Suhendroyono, A.A.G.R. Gunawarman, P. Maulidimas, Comprehensive analysis of accessible tourism and its case study in Indonesia. J. Environ. Manag. Tour. **13**, 995 (2022). https://doi.org/10.14505/jemt.v13.4(60).08
16. UNWTO International Network of Sustainable Tourism Observatories (INSTO), Webinar on Accessibility: Measuring the Economic Impact of Accessible Tourism within the European Union and Beyond (2021, 7th September). https://www.unwto.org/event/technical-insto-webinar-on-accessibility
17. D. Denyer, D. Tranfield, Producing a systematic review, in *The SAGE Handbook Of Organizational Research Methods*, ed. by D.A. Buchanan, A. Bryman (SAGE Publications, 2009), p. 671
18. R. Yung, C. Khoo-Lattimore, New realities: a systematic literature review on virtual reality and augmented reality in tourism research. Curr. Issues Tour. **22**, 2056 (2019). https://doi.org/10.1080/13683500.2017.1417359
19. D. Agapito, The senses in tourism design: a bibliometric review. Ann. Tour. Res. **83**, 102934 (2020). https://doi.org/10.1016/j.annals.2020.102934
20. S. Darcy, Inherent complexity: disability, accessible tourism and accommodation information preferences. Tour. Manag. **31**, 816 (2010). https://doi.org/10.1016/j.tourman.2009.08.010
21. S. Darcy, B. Cameron, S. Pegg, Accessible tourism and sustainability: a discussion and case study. J. Sustain. Tour. **18**, 515 (2010). https://doi.org/10.1080/09669581003690668
22. M. Agovino, M. Casaccia, A, Garofalo, K. Marchesano, Tourism and disability in Italy. Limits and opportunities. Tour. Manag. Perspect **23**, 58 (2017). https://doi.org/10.1016/j.tmp.2017.05.001
23. T. Domínguez, J.A. Fraiz, E. Alén, Economic profitability of accessible tourism for the tourism sector in Spain. Tour. Econ. **19**, 1385 (2013). https://doi.org/10.5367/te.2013.0246
24. J. Bowtell, Assessing the value and market attractiveness of the accessible tourism industry in Europe: a focus on major travel and leisure companies. J. Tour. Futures **1**, 203 (2015). https://doi.org/10.1108/jtf-03-2015-0012
25. B. Gillovic, A, McIntosh, C. Cockburn-Wootten, S. Darcy, Experiences of tourists with intellectual disabilities: a phenomenological approach. J. Hosp. Tour. Manag. **48**, 155 (2021). https://doi.org/10.1016/j.jhtm.2021.06.003
26. J.Y. Chung, H. Lee, Desired recreation companionship and travel behaviour of people with disabilities. Asia Pac. J. Tour. Res. **24**, 314 (2019). https://doi.org/10.1080/10941665.2018.1564343
27. F. Ali, L. Cain, T.S. Legendre, L. Wu, The intersection of technology, accessible tourism and tourists with intellectual disabilities: proposing a novel conceptual framework. J. Hosp. Tour. Res. (2022). https://doi.org/10.1177/10963480221142499
28. F. Rahmafitria, P. Dirgahayani, H.P.H. Putro, A. Rosyidie, D. Hudalah, Tourism accessibility in protected islands: the case of the Komodo National Park, Indonesia. Tour. Rev. (2022). https://doi.org/10.1108/TR-03-2022-0110

29. A. Moura, C. Eusébio, E. Devile, The 'why' and 'what for' of participation in tourism activities: travel motivations of people with disabilities. Curr. Issues Tour. **26**, 941 (2023). https://doi.org/10.1080/13683500.2022.2044292
30. A, Gassiot Melian, L. Prats, L. Coromina, The perceived value of accessibility in religious sites—do disabled and non-disabled travellers behave differently? Tour. Rev. **71**, 105 (2016). https://doi.org/10.1108/tr-11-2015-0057
31. J.J. Nigg, M. Peters, The evolution of ICTs in accessible tourism: a stakeholder collaboration analysis. J. Hosp. Tour. Manag. **52**, 287 (2022). https://doi.org/10.1016/j.jhtm.2022.07.007
32. A.F.A. Moura, E. Kastenholz, A.M.S. Pereira, Accessible tourism and its benefits for coping with stress. J. Policy Res. Tour. Leisure Events **10**, 241 (2018). https://doi.org/10.4324/9780429290077-5
33. M. Allan, Accessible tourism in Jordan: travel constrains and motivations. Eur. J. Tour. Res. **10**, 109 (2015). https://doi.org/10.54055/ejtr.v10i.182
34. S. Mahmoudzadeh, N.K. Sarjaz, Environmental barriers to tourism development for people with disabilities. Acta Turistica **30**, 87 (2018). https://doi.org/10.22598/at/2018.30.1.87
35. A. De Pascale, M. Meleddu, T. Abbate, M. Pellicano, M. Is there a gender gap in the propensity to travel of people with disabilities? J. Travel Res. **62**, 517 (2023). https://doi.org/10.1177/00472875211073976
36. V. Vigolo, *Older Tourist Behavior and Marketing Tools* (Springer International Publising, Cham, 2017)
37. Y.K.P. Wan, W.S.S. Lo, M.E. Eddy-U, Perceived constraints and negotiation strategies by elderly tourists when visiting heritage sites. Leis Stud. **41**, 703 (2022). https://doi.org/10.1080/02614367.2022.2066710
38. S.F. Gregory, Diving with dignity? Older women scuba divers, constraints and accessible tourism on the Great Barrier Reef. Ann. Leis. Res. (2022). https://doi.org/10.1080/11745398.2022.2041449
39. M. Eddy-U, T.I.W. Kong, Y.K.P. Wan, Senior travelers to integrated resorts: preferences, consuming behaviors and barriers. J. Qual. Assur. Hosp. Tour. **21**, 297 (2020). https://doi.org/10.1080/1528008x.2019.1659209
40. P. Teixeira, C, Eusébio, L. Teixeira, Website accessibility in the hospitality industry: a study in the central region of Portugal. Int. J. Tour. Policy **11**, 222 (2021). https://doi.org/10.1504/ijtp.2021.118666
41. K.L. Lam, C.-S. Chan, M. Peters, Understanding technological contributions to accessible tourism from the perspective of destination design for visually impaired visitors in Hong Kong. J. Dest. Mark. Manag. **17**, 100434 (2020). https://doi.org/10.1016/j.jdmm.2020.100434
42. E. Devile, E. Kastenholz, Accessible tourism experiences: the voice of people with visual disabilities. J. Policy Res. Tour. Leis. Events **10**, 265 (2018). https://doi.org/10.1080/19407963.2018.1470183
43. A.J. McIntosh, The hidden side of travel: epilepsy and tourism. Ann. Tour. Res. **81**, 102856 (2020). https://doi.org/10.1016/j.annals.2019.102856
44. D. Freund, M. Cerdan Chiscano, G. Hernandez-Maskivker, M. Guix, A. Iñesta, M. Castelló, Enhancing the hospitality customer experience of families with children on the autism spectrum disorder. Int. J. Tour. Res. **21**, 606 (2019). https://doi.org/10.1002/jtr.2284
45. E. Nyman, K. Westin, D. Carson, Tourism destination choice sets for families with wheelchair-bound children. Tour. Rec. Res. **43**, 26 (2018). https://doi.org/10.1080/02508281.2017.1362172
46. E. Figueiredo, C. Eusébio, E. Kastenholz, How *diverse* are tourists with disabilities? A pilot study on accessible leisure tourism experiences in Portugal. Int. J. Tour. Res. **14**, 531 (2012). https://doi.org/10.1002/jtr.1913
47. D. Buhalis, E. Michopoulou, Information-enabled tourism destination marketing: addressing the accessibility market. Curr. Issues Tour. **14**, 145 (2011). https://doi.org/10.1080/13683501003653361
48. A. Marasco, B. Balbi, Designing accessible experiences for heritage visitors through virtual reality. e-Rev. Tour. Res. **17**, 426 (2019)

49. E. Michopoulou, D. Buhalis, Information provision for challenging markets: the case of the accessibility requiring market in the context of tourism. Inf. Manag. **50**, 229 (2013). https://doi.org/10.1016/j.im.2013.04.001
50. A. Zajadacz, Sources of tourist information used by deaf people. Case study: the polish deaf community. Curr. Issues Tour. **17**, 434 (2014). https://doi.org/10.1080/13683500.2012.725713
51. A. Naniopoulos, P. Tsalis, D. Nalmpantis, An effort to develop accessible tourism in Greece and Turkey: the MEDRA project approach. J. Tour. Futures **2**, 56 (2016). https://doi.org/10.1108/jtf-03-2015-0009
52. J. Small, S. Darcy, T. Packer, The embodied tourist experiences of people with vision impairment: management implications beyond the visual gaze. Tour Manag. **33**, 941 (2012). https://doi.org/10.1016/j.tourman.2011.09.015
53. S. Darcy, Developing sustainable approaches to accessible accommodation information provision: a foundation for strategic knowledge management. Tour. Rec. Res. **36**, 141 (2011). https://doi.org/10.1080/02508281.2011.11081315

Chapter 3
The Perspective of Digital Ecosystems for Accessible Tourism: Conceptual and Operational Issues

Fabio Cassia, Alessandro Bigi, and Marta Ugolini

Abstract The digital ecosystems logic has the potential to enhance the current understanding of accessible tourism, explaining how valuable tourism experiences for people with access requirements are co-created by multiple actors. This chapter aims to shed further light on this perspective and its conceptual and practical implications. The chapter first presents the theoretical underpinnings of service ecosystems, moving then to digital ecosystems, and the role of digital platforms. These concepts are then applied to tourism experiences in general and to accessible tourism experiences in particular. Finally, reflections on the conditions for properly functioning digital ecosystems for accessible tourism are presented.

Keywords Digital ecosystems · Accessible tourism · Value co-creation · Technological platforms · Barriers

3.1 Introduction to the Logic of Service Ecosystems

The concept of service ecosystems is well-established in service research nowadays, reflecting the awareness that value-creation processes involve a system of multiple, co-evolving actors [1]. A recent literature review of academic studies on service ecosystems highlighted that the concept appeared for the first time in 2003 but gained popularity about one decade later [2], after Vargo, Lusch, and Akaka published their initial, well-known articles on this topic [3, 4]. Since then, the volume of academic articles on service ecosystems has quickly and steadily increased [2].

A service ecosystem is "a relatively self-contained, self-adjusting system of resource-integrating actors connected by shared institutional arrangements and

F. Cassia (✉) · M. Ugolini
University of Verona, Verona, Italy
e-mail: fabio.cassia@univr.it

A. Bigi
Royal Docks School of Business and Law, University of East London, London, UK

F. Cassia et al. (eds.), *Accessible Tourism in the Digital Ecosystem*,
SpringerBriefs in Applied Sciences and Technology,
https://doi.org/10.1007/978-3-031-38782-1_3

mutual value creation" [5, pp. 10–11]. This conceptualization points out that, in service ecosystems, the focus is on the service logic, meaning that service (exchange) is at the base of value co-creation in service ecosystems. Service means the application of an actor's knowledge and skills for the benefit of another actor. Value is then co-created through service-for-service exchanges among the actors [6].

The current understanding of value co-creation in service ecosystems draws on the service-dominant logic (S-D logic) [7, 8]. One of the most important tenets of S-D Logic is the distinction between operand and operant resources. Operand resources are those upon which an act is performed, while operant resources—such as actors' knowledge and skills—are those that act upon operand and other operant resources [8]. Technology itself is conceptualized as an operant resource by S-D Logic [9]. Therefore, the ecosystems' actors act as integrators of resources and co-create value through their service exchange. In sum, all actors act as both providers and beneficiaries of service and, as a beneficiary, each actor phenomenologically determines value, or the perceived "benefit, an increase in the well-being of a particular actor" [10, p. 57]. For a comprehensive and more detailed review of S-D Logic; see Vargo et al. [11] or Akaka et al. [12].

In service ecosystems, shared institutions are a particular type of operant resource that plays a fundamental role in driving interactions and are needed for value co-creation. Institutions are intended as common norms and rules which act as (either formal or informal) coordinating mechanisms among the ecosystem's actors. Institutions "provide the building blocks for the increasingly complex and interrelated resource-integration activities in nested and overlapping ecosystems organized around shared purposes" [12, p. 382]. More precisely, the definition of service ecosystems mentioned before refers to institutional arrangements, which are to be intended as "assemblages of interrelated institutions, which can contain technological, sociological, cultural, and economic structures" [12, p. 381]. Such institutional arrangements both influence and are influenced by value co-creation so that they are dynamically renegotiated and recombined [9]. Interactions among actors not only contribute to value co-creation but also maintain and change institutions, leading to innovations in technology and markets [13].

Another fundamental contribution of the service ecosystems perspective lies in its ability to enable a deeper and more complex understanding of value co-creation by acknowledging the multiple interactions and influences taking place at multiple levels (beyond the recurrent focus on the customer-provider dyad). In detail, service ecosystems can be observed from different intertwined levels, known as "macro," "meso," and "micro." The macro-level refers to the broader level such as nations; the meso-level indicates structures such as markets, industries, and brand communities, while the micro-level focuses on individuals and dyads [12, 14]. Finally, service ecosystems continuously and dynamically evolve through their value co-creation activities with the aim of preserving their viability. As highlighted by the definition introduced at the beginning of this paragraph, service ecosystems are also "self-adjusting," meaning that each iteration of the value creation process leads to a reconfiguration of the whole ecosystem [4].

3.2 The Evolutions Enabled by Digital Technologies and the Digital Ecosystems

Studies about service ecosystems have noted that the service logic is essential to understand the digital transformation of actors and markets [15] and have conceptually pointed out the key role of technology as an operant resource [16]. Drawing on these premises, some authors have investigated how digital technologies can facilitate resource integration and value co-creation among actors [17]. Not surprisingly, this research stream is rapidly gaining popularity. Gölgeci et al.'s [2] recent literature review of academic studies on service ecosystems found that one of the four main themes was related to technology as a change trigger in service ecosystems comprising aspects such as digitalization, the Internet of things, and business model innovation.

Starting with these premises, digital service ecosystems have been conceptualized as service ecosystems supported by or created around a digital infrastructure. Such technology facilitates value co-creation in the ecosystem and also enables actors weakly tied to the ecosystems to participate in the co-creation processes [18]. The digital infrastructure takes the form of a digital platform that facilitates actors' engagement to integrate their resources [19]. Hence, a specific stream of research on business ecosystems has even specifically conceptualized platform ecosystems defined as those created around technological platforms, which are usually owned by a focal firm [1, 20]. More broadly, one or more actors (a focal firm for example) play a key role in driving the digital transformation of the ecosystem and providing the digital platform [18, 19].

By facilitating and enhancing intra- and inter-organizational interactions among the actors, digital technologies have the potential to concretely improve value co-creation and actors' well-being in multiple ways. In detail, some of the most relevant evolutions supported by digital service ecosystems are the following:

- omnichannel service experience, which emerges from the co-creation of seamless customer journeys along multiple touchpoints and interactions with multiple actors (such as different service providers). In this context, the integration of real-time data from the ecosystems' actors supports the effective and efficient co-creation of seamless service experiences [21].
- data-driven decision-making, which improves the quality of the actors' decisions using insights from the continuous collection and analysis of large amounts of data provided by different actors and at different points in the ecosystem [22].
- automation, which draws on shared data and information to support chatbots, robots, and other forms of automation to increase customer experience [23].
- personalization of service experiences, which makes use of individual data, information about customers (and other ecosystems' actors), and techniques such as machine learning to design personalized service experiences within the ecosystem [24, 25].
- co-creation of new services, as highlighted by the stream of studies about digital servitization. According to this perspective, digital technologies not only improve

the co-creation of existing services but can also lead to the (co)development and configuration of new services [26].

Digital platforms have the potential to enhance the value co-created by the ecosystem. At the same time, the introduction of new technologies, such as digital platforms, implies maintenance and change in the existing institutional arrangements among the co-creating actors [9]. As a result of factors such as actors' different levels of digital maturity, the transition from a pre-digitalized to a digitalized service ecosystem is not necessarily smooth and successful [18]. More broadly, the formation of new institutional arrangements in the digitalized service ecosystem requires shared intentions among the actors. Such shared intentions are based on compatible sub-plans, mutual responsiveness, interdependence, and knowledge of the conditions needed for the emergence of shared intentions from individual intentions [27]. A digitalized service ecosystem does not necessarily result in value creation but can also result in value destruction. Schulz et al. [28] provided an example of such an occasion when discussing a case of the introduction of an app to support service ecosystems for smart mobility which led to both value creation and value co-destruction because of insufficient resource integration among the actors.

3.3 The Application of the Service Ecosystem Perspective to Tourism Experiences

The service ecosystem logic has gained increasing popularity in tourism studies, which is not surprising considering its ability to reflect the main characteristics of the tourism industries and of the co-creation of valuable tourism experiences:

- the (co)creation of tourism experiences requires extensive collaboration and interaction among a wide number of actors, including public and private ones and tourists themselves, thus involving an ecosystem of actors [29].
- the actors participating in the (co)creation of tourism experiences belong to multiple service ecosystems simultaneously [30]. Broadly speaking, "the tourism ecosystem consists of micro-experiences across online travel agencies, accommodation, transport and destination activities" [25, p. 491]. The destination ecosystem—the most studied tourism ecosystem—overlaps with other ecosystems (e.g., distribution channels) and has interactions outside the core geographical area [29]. Therefore, the identification of the actors contributing to the co-creation of specific tourism experiences is not immediately clear, which is reflected in the ecosystem's absence of clearly defined boundaries.
- the number, types, and characteristics of the actors participating in the co-creation of tourism experiences are continuously evolving, making tourism ecosystems dynamic, and adjusting to changing scenarios. Technological advancements have enabled both new actors (e.g., online intermediaries) and a wider array of already existing actors to participate in the co-creation processes. The prominent role of

technology is reflected in the concept of the smart tourism ecosystem which is defined as a "tourism system that takes advantage of smart technology in creating, managing and delivering intelligent touristic services/experiences and is characterized by intensive information sharing and value co-creation" [29, p. 560].
- Co-creating valuable experiences for tourists (or the achievement of the so-called tourist experience quality) is highly complex. Unsatisfactory resource integration in one of the ecosystems participating in the experience co-creation (e.g., the transportation ecosystem) [30], as well as inconsistencies across actors in delivered quality and the information provided to tourists [31], may compromise the overall value or well-being experienced by tourists.

Available tourism literature adopting the service ecosystems logic has investigated co-creation at the macro-, meso-, and micro-levels [32]. However, the vast majority of extant literature has taken the meso-perspective of destinations, considering Destination Management Organizations (DMOs) as the focal actors aiming at coordinating and optimizing the offerings of a destination's multiple service providers (for a comprehensive review; see Gao et al. [33]). This branch of studies has particularly emphasized the role of digital ecosystems in proposing the concept of smart destinations [34]. Such ecosystems require the use of digital platforms to foster collaboration among the actors and involve tourists in experience co-creation. Several digital platforms have been proposed for this purpose:

- websites and portals, including those promoted by DMOs or by other actors of the destination. These platforms take the form of Destination Management Systems, which combine the front-end websites or portals used by tourists with intranets and extranets to facilitate collaboration and coordination among the destination's stakeholders involved in service provision [35]. The DMO of San Francisco, for example, uses its website to collect information from tourists, integrate it with information from other actors, and co-create personalized itineraries using a recommender system [36]. Another example is provided by Cabiddu et al. [37], who studied the website promoted by an inbound tour operator, Portale Sardegna (Sardinia, Italy), which established an Internet-enabled network of affiliated hotels with the intent of promoting a new value proposition, called Open Voucher.
- mobile applications. Barile et al. [38] analyzed the case of a tourism app, Smartour, created in the city of Salerno (Italy) to bring together the services offered by actors in the destination. The application proposed tourist routes in the city, while including integrated information in the routes about the timetable of transport services, the total costs of the attractions, etc. In addition, the routes suggested to tourists were personalized based on their preferences collected (if authorized) from tourists' profiles on social media through tourists' involvement in gamified activities.
- social media. Ge and Gretzel [39] investigated co-creating actors and activities on Weibo, finding that several destination actors, such as DMOs, museums and other tourism attractions, accommodation providers, and local administrations, as well as tourists, contributed to tourism experience co-creation and sharing.

Similar studies were conducted on other social media platforms, such as Facebook, Instagram, and Twitter [40].

- co-creation tools. Google and other digital platforms have developed tools to support co-creation and sharing of user-generated content to large audience. In detail, they enabled users (both customer and suppliers) to enrich online contents working together with mutual benefits. For example, Purbasari et al. [41] investigated the use of Google My Business (GMB) as a tourism promotion medium identifying it as a successful tool for content co-creation.

To accomplish their aims, digital platforms can combine several functionalities, including those facilitating travel planning and bookings (flights, tickets for attractions, accommodations, etc.), chatrooms, chatbots, forums, blogs, interactive maps and location-based services, linking to third-party platforms (such as TripAdvisor), sharing of itineraries planned by other tourists, personalized and real-time information about the availability of services, and many others. When properly designed, these functionalities satisfy tourists' informational, communicational, transactional, and relational needs [35].

Recent studies further reflect on the future role of artificial intelligence in shaping co-creation within destination service ecosystems. Artificial intelligence could impact access to relevant information (DMO-provided robots could guide tourists through the destination), personalization of the experience (artificial intelligence could create offers and autonomously book the related services based on tourist's preferences), and integration of physical and virtual experiences of a destination [42].

The availability of an engagement platform is fundamental but not sufficient to enable a destination's actors to co-create valuable tourism experiences. Drawing on the service ecosystems view and lexicon, shared intention is a prerequisite for the formation of new institutional arrangements such as those related to the adoption of a new platform for resource integration and value co-creation [27]. Moreover, tourism literature acknowledges that some conditions have to be satisfied for successful platform-based value co-creation, such as the actors' willingness to cooperate and share information, the availability of adequate resources including time for daily operations (e.g., daily updates of information in the platform), and the DMO's ability to coordinate the system [35]. Ongoing debate suggests that both private and public sector organizations should play a role in setting up ecosystem coordination mechanisms to develop and sustain effective coopetitive relationships. In particular, "in tourism destination service ecosystems, the creation of artifacts (formal documents informing the common vision and guiding principles) developed by a public sector organization facilitate collective decision-making and overcome competitive tensions within private organizations" [43, p. 453]. Data policy issues (including privacy and security), technological culture and capabilities, as well as ethical issues related to the use of technological platforms also need to be addressed by the involved actors for the proper functioning of the ecosystem [44].

The service ecosystem logic has proved valuable for understanding the co-creation of tourism experiences at the destination (or meso) level, specifically for the co-creation supported by digital platforms. However, in addition to the limitations discussed before (e.g., limits in the availability of technological skills), additional matters of concern should be emphasized. Tourism experiences emerge from co-creation processes involving multiple actors, who are simultaneously part of different ecosystems, with the tourist as the beneficiary of the co-created value or well-being. Co-creating actors are often unaware of being part of the same ecosystem and have only a partial view of the interconnected service ecosystems that a tourist is involved in during travel [30]. Moreover, the ecosystems which are relevant for the co-creation of a specific tourism experience extend beyond the boundaries of the destination, such as the transportation ecosystem that makes it possible for the tourist to reach the destination.

The identification of relevant ecosystems and their actors requires following the Tourism Customer Journey (TCJ) perspective, which involves tracing the complete path of a tourist, including all the phases and interactions a person goes through when traveling for tourism purposes [45]. The TCJ comprises four main stages—destination choice and trip design, outbound trip, staying at the destination, transfer to another destination, or return home—which can be articulated in dozens of activities and interactions and involve dozens of actors, from transport and accommodation providers to municipalities and residents of the destination [46], as well as companies typically assigned to other industries (such as medical services providers and retailers) [29]. In sum, the application of the service ecosystems logic to tourism enables a comprehensive understanding of the complexity of the processes behind the co-creation of valuable tourism experiences.

3.4 Digital Ecosystems and Accessible Tourism

By definition, accessible tourism requires collaboration among multiple actors [47]. Accessible tourism is a "form of tourism that involves collaborative processes between stakeholders that enables people with access requirements, including mobility, vision, hearing and cognitive dimensions of access, to function independently and with equity and dignity through the delivery of universally designed tourism products, services and environments" [48, p. 10]. In other words, the co-creation of valuable tourism experiences for people with access requirements emerges from resource integration among cooperating actors in service ecosystems. During each stage of the customer journey for tourists with access requirements, various actors play a role in shaping the overall tourist experience by either delivering or not delivering on expectations. These actors form the tourism service ecosystem (or a combination of ecosystems) from the tourist's perspective and have to work together to co-create value for the customer. However, there is often a lack of coordination among the actors involved in co-creating the tourism experience and sometimes even a lack of awareness of belonging to the same ecosystem. Each actor tends to perceive only a portion of the tourist customer journey and fails to gain a comprehensive understanding of the formation of customer experiences.

Recent work has identified multiple barriers that hinder the effective co-creation of tourism experiences for tourists with disabilities, thus limiting the formation of tourists' well-being. Such barriers can be classified into the following types [46]:

- Informational barriers refer to the difficulties faced by individuals with disabilities when trying to independently evaluate and choose transportation, accommodations, holiday itineraries, or other activities. Despite the abundance of general information available for these services, the specific informational needs of people with disabilities result in higher levels of complexity. For instance, even when information about tourism services is accessible, it can still be challenging to verify its accuracy and suitability for their needs [49].
- Architectural barriers refer to the multiple challenges faced by individuals with disabilities while on holiday, such as accessing transportation, navigating different locations, and using sidewalks [50]. Some characteristics of tourism attractions can make the removal of architectural barriers more complex. For example, archaeological areas and historical buildings are subject to strict regulations and constraints. In these cases, all interventions must be evaluated and authorized by specific authorities in charge of the conservation of cultural, historical, and natural heritage.
- Economic barriers refer to budget constraints experienced in some specific situations. The organization of temporary events, for example, is generally characterized by tight budgets and even minor interventions to remove access barriers, when not planned from the beginning of the budgeting process, can incur significant costs. In these cases, it becomes difficult for the organizers to find additional resources.
- Political barriers refer to the fact that, despite political discourse promoting the elimination of architectural barriers, political actions are in many cases driven by immediate priorities and short-term thinking [51].
- Cultural barriers refer to the lack of understanding and respect people show toward individuals with disabilities and are reflected in behaviors such as the improper use of parking spots for people with disabilities. These barriers also include tourism and hospitality personnel's lack of proper education about the needs of people with disabilities [52]. An additional cultural barrier is that a large share of the population may not show sufficient appreciation of accessibility interventions because they think that accessibility is a problem limited to a few categories of people. They do not think that all people benefit from interventions aimed at improving the accessibility of specific tourism attractions and experiences.
- Planning barriers refer to the inaccurate planning of interventions to remove barriers, which does not consider all possible future user experience scenarios. For example, the organizers of a cultural event (such as a music concert) may design and reserve some specific areas that are easily accessible for wheelchair users. However, if, during the event, other people in front seats decide to stand up, the view of the wheelchair users will be obstructed.
- Relational barriers refer to the difficulties in establishing relationships with people with disabilities because of biased views and stereotypes. Tourism service

providers, for example, may hold stereotypical beliefs that all individuals with disabilities have similar characteristics and needs [47].

- Technological barriers refer to the rapid and continuous changes in communication technologies, often increasing the digital divide for people with disabilities [52].
- Entrepreneurial myopia barriers reflect tourism and hospitality entrepreneurs' inability to perceive the remarkable size and value of the tourism market for people with disabilities [53].

Technology can contribute to solving, at least partially, the mentioned barriers. A detailed literature review by Teixeira et al. [54] indicated the usefulness of several technologies for this purpose. Some of them, such as websites, are already in their maturity phase, while others, such as mobile applications, are in their growth stage. In addition, there are many technologies in their embryonic stage, such as virtual reality, image recognition software, cloud technologies, and online multimedia material [54]. From the ecosystem perspective, the focus is on understanding how digital platforms can contribute to overcoming the barriers reviewed before and increasing coordination among actors to co-create high-quality experiences for tourists with disabilities [52, 55]. The European Network for Accessible Tourism (ENAT), which is supported by the European Commission, carries a number of ongoing and past (since 2009) projects and good practices based on technological platforms to support the emergence of ecosystems for accessible tourism on its website (https://www.accessibletourism.org/?i=enat.en.projects). Moreover, new platform-based ecosystems for accessible tourism are being promoted by firms and startups like Willeasy, which calls itself the "first digital accessibility ecosystem that creates connections between people with special needs and the right facilities to best accommodate them" (https://www.willeasy.net/project/en/home-english/). Willeasy collects data on the accessibility of places, events, and facilities making them available to people with special needs with the support of artificial intelligence.

Despite a growing number of initiatives to facilitate the emergence of digital ecosystems for accessible tourism, extant research suggests that much remains to be done. An analysis of the city of Porto (Portugal) revealed that it is overall an accessible destination but also showed that accessibility was not properly conveyed on technological platforms. Even the official destination and attractions' websites did not comply with the minimum standard of accessibility (i.e., information about accessibility was not accessible). Even the website Accessible Itineraries contained only generic and outdated content [56]. Therefore, as outlined by the literature on digital ecosystems, it should be remarked that technological platforms cannot by themselves guarantee effective value co-creation and that their adoption can sometimes even result in value co-destruction.

Shared awareness and intention among the involved actors is fundamental for properly functioning digital ecosystems and all of the co-creating actors have to be equipped with the needed resources (knowledge and skills) to participate in successful resource integration. For these reasons, educational activities about how individuals with disabilities experience tourism are a necessary condition for co-creation. The ongoing project Feelit (https://feelit.infoproject.eu/), focusing on tourism for deaf and hard-of-hearing people, aims to create a virtual reality and personal computer 3D game for tourism providers to understand how it feels to be a visitor with hearing impairments in a foreign country. Similarly, tourists should be equipped with the needed knowledge and skills (i.e., with the necessary operant resources) to take part to experience co-creation, starting from knowledge and skills to the access and use of engaging platforms (websites, applications, or other platforms).

In addition, the emergence of digital ecosystems for accessible tourism requires time and effort because it implies a "non-linear process in which all actors engage in institutional work and co-create institutions through multiple iterations of institutional developments until common templates emerge that reflect shared conceptions of problems and solutions" [13, p. 69]. The overview of past projects (such as those described on the ENAT portal) working to facilitate the emergence of digital ecosystems seems to indicate that shared intention and coordination mechanisms are essential to ensure that the ecosystem becomes self-adjusting and continues to "exist" and co-create value over time. For this purpose, some authors have proposed that the digital ecosystems for accessible tourism should be led by public authorities in charge at the territorial level, being it a city, a region, or a country [46]. On this point, Shahzalal and Elgammal [47] argued that collaboration between actors, government agencies with regulatory powers, and key stakeholders can result in higher actor engagement in the ecosystem's activities directed at the development of sustainable tourism. Other studies [e.g., 35] have proposed that DMOs (whenever they have been established) at national, regional, and even local levels should act as leaders of such initiatives through destination marketing systems. However, there is an urgent need for more empirical research to better understand the conditions required for well-functioning digital ecosystems for accessible tourism to emerge and develop over time.

References

1. L. Aarikka-Stenroos, P. Ritala, Network management in the era of ecosystems: systematic review and management framework. Ind. Mark. Manage. **67**, 23 (2017)
2. I. Gölgeci, I. Ali, P. Ritala, A. Arslan, A bibliometric review of service ecosystems research: current status and future directions. J. Bus. Ind. Market. **37**(4), 841 (2022)
3. S.L. Vargo, M.A. Akaka, Value cocreation and service systems (re) formation: a service ecosystems view. Serv. Sci. **4**(3), 207 (2012)
4. S. L. Vargo, R. F. Lusch, It's all B2B … and beyond: toward a systems perspective of the market. Ind. Market. Manag. **40**(2), 181 (2011)
5. S.L. Vargo, R.F. Lusch, Institutions and axioms: an extension and update of service-dominant logic. J. Acad. Mark. Sci. **44**(1), 5 (2016)
6. R. F. Lusch, S. L. Vargo, *The Service-Dominant Logic of Marketing: Dialog, Debate, and Directions* (M.E. Sharpe, Armonk, New York, 2014)
7. S.L. Vargo, R.F. Lusch, Service-dominant logic: continuing the evolution. J. Acad. Mark. Sci. **36**(1), 1 (2008)
8. S.L. Vargo, R.F. Lusch, Evolving to a new dominant logic for marketing. J. Mark. **68**(1), 1 (2004)

9. M.A. Akaka, K. Koskela-Huotari, S.L. Vargo, in *Handbook of Service Science*, vol. II, ed. by P.P. Maglio et al. (Springer, New York, 2019), p.641
10. R.F. Lusch, S.L. Vargo, *Service-Dominant Logic: Premises, Perspectives, Possibilities* (Cambridge University Press, New York, 2014)
11. S.L. Vargo, K. Koskela-Huotari, J. Vink, in *The Routledge Handbook of Service Research Insights and Ideas*. ed. by E. Bridges, K. Fowler (Routledge, New York, 2020), p.3
12. M.A. Akaka, K. Koskela-Huotari, S.L. Vargo, Formalizing service-dominant logic as a general theory of markets: taking stock and moving forward. AMS Review **11**, 375 (2021)
13. S.L. Vargo, H. Wieland, M.A. Akaka, Innovation through institutionalization: a service ecosystems perspective. Ind. Mark. Manage. **44**, 63 (2015)
14. M.V. Ciasullo, O. Troisi, M. Grimaldi, D. Leone, Multi-level governance for sustainable innovation in smart communities: an ecosystems approach. Int. Entrepreneurship Manag. J. **16**(4), 1167 (2020)
15. I.C. Ng, S.L. Vargo, Service-dominant logic, service ecosystems and institutions: an editorial. J. Serv. Manag. **29**(4), 518 (2018)
16. M.A. Akaka, S.L. Vargo, Technology as an operant resource in service (eco) systems. IseB **12**(3), 367 (2014)
17. M. Balaji, S.K. Roy, Value co-creation with Internet of things technology in the retail industry. J. Mark. Manag. **33**(1–2), 7 (2017)
18. A. Sklyar, C. Kowalkowski, D. Sörhammar, B. Tronvoll, Resource integration through digitalisation: a service ecosystem perspective. J. Mark. Manag. **35**(11–12), 974 (2019)
19. K. Storbacka, R.J. Brodie, T. Böhmann, P.P. Maglio, S. Nenonen, Actor engagement as a microfoundation for value co-creation. J. Bus. Res. **69**(8), 3008 (2016)
20. H. Peng, Y. Lu, S. Gupta, Promoting value emergence through digital platform ecosystems: perspectives on resource integration in China. Technol. Forecast. Soc. Chang. **189**, 122338 (2023)
21. L.S. Dalenogare, M.-A. Le Dain, G.B. Benitez, N.F. Ayala, A.G. Frank, Multichannel digital service delivery and service ecosystems: the role of data integration within smart product-service systems. Technol. Forecast. Soc. Chang. **183**, 121894 (2022)
22. F. Cassia, F. Magno, Data-driven use of cross-border e-commerce platforms and export performance: the mediating role of foreign market knowledge acquisition. Sinergie Ital. J. Manag. **40**(1), 131 (2022)
23. H. Shin, A critical review of robot research and future research opportunities: adopting a service ecosystem perspective. Int. J. Contemp. Hosp. Manag. **34**(6), 2337 (2022)
24. V. Kumar, V. Chattaraman, C. Neghina, B. Skiera, L. Aksoy, A. Buoye, J. Henseler, Data-driven services marketing in a connected world. J. Serv. Manag. **24**(3), 330 (2013)
25. D. Buhalis, T. Harwood, V. Bogicevic, G. Viglia, S. Beldona, C. Hofacker, Technological disruptions in services: lessons from tourism and hospitality. J. Serv. Manag. **30**(4), 484 (2019)
26. B. Struyf, S. Galvani, P. Matthyssens, R. Bocconcelli, Toward a multilevel perspective on digital servitization. Int. J. Oper. Prod. Manag. **41**(5), 668 (2021)
27. M. Taillard, L.D. Peters, J. Pels, C. Mele, The role of shared intentions in the emergence of service ecosystems. J. Bus. Res. **69**(8), 2972 (2016)
28. T. Schulz, S. Zimmermann, M. Böhm, H. Gewald, H. Krcmar, Value co-creation and co-destruction in service ecosystems: The case of the Reach Now app. Technol. Forecast. Soc. Chang. **170**, 120926 (2021)
29. U. Gretzel, H. Werthner, C. Koo, C. Lamsfus, Conceptual foundations for understanding smart tourism ecosystems. Comput. Hum. Behav. **50**, 558 (2015)
30. C. Baccarani, F. Cassia, Evaluating the outcomes of service ecosystems: The interplay between ecosystem well-being and customer well-being. TQM J. **29**(6), 834 (2017)
31. A. Bigi, F. Cassia, M.M. Ugolini, Who killed food tourism? Unaware cannibalism in online conversations about traveling in Italy. Br. Food J. **124**(2), 573 (2022)
32. F. Simeoni, F. Cassia, From vehicle suppliers to value co-creators: the evolving role of Italian motorhome manufacturers. Curr. Issue Tour. **22**(2), 218 (2019)

33. Y. Gao, Q. Zhang, X. Xu, F. Jia, Z. Lin, Service design for the destination tourism service ecosystem: a review and extension. Asia Pacific J. Tour. Res. **27**(3), 225 (2022)
34. E. Sorokina, Y. Wang, A. Fyall, P. Lugosi, E. Torres, T. Jung, Constructing a smart destination framework: a destination marketing organization perspective. J. Destin. Mark. Manag. **23**, 100688 (2022)
35. J. Estêvão, L. Teixeira, M.J. Carneiro, The relevance of destination management systems' functionalities: a model based on stakeholders' view. J. Organ. Comput. Electron. Commer. **32**(1), 21 (2022)
36. F. Femenia-Serra, B. Neuhofer, J.A. Ivars-Baidal, Towards a conceptualisation of smart tourists and their role within the smart destination scenario. Serv. Ind. J. **39**(2), 109 (2019)
37. F. Cabiddu, T.-W. Lui, G. Piccoli, Managing value co-creation in the tourism industry. Ann. Tour. Res. **42**, 86 (2013)
38. S. Barile, M.V. Ciasullo, O. Troisi, D. Sarno, The role of technology and institutions in tourism service ecosystems: findings from a case study. TQM J. **29**(6), 811 (2017)
39. J. Ge, U. Gretzel, A taxonomy of value co-creation on Weibo–a communication perspective. Int. J. Contemp. Hosp. Manag. **30**(4), 2075 (2018)
40. D. Buhalis, M. Foerste, SoCoMo marketing for travel and tourism: Empowering co-creation of value. J. Destin. Mark. Manag. **4**(3), 151 (2015)
41. A. Purbasari, G.P. Maryono, F. Mulyanto, W. Gusdya, Utilization of Google my business as a tourism promotion media using local search engine optimization. IAIC Trans. Sustain. Digital Innov. (ITSDI) **2**(2), 169 (2021)
42. L. Grundner, B. Neuhofer, The bright and dark sides of artificial intelligence: a futures perspective on tourist destination experiences. J. Destin. Mark. Manag. **19**, 100511 (2021)
43. K. Picaud-Bello, E. Stevens, L.M. Cloutier, L. Renard, Coordinating service ecosystems for innovation: the case of tourism destination innovation projects. Ind. Mark. Manage. **106**, 444 (2022)
44. M. Sigala, New technologies in tourism: from multi-disciplinary to anti-disciplinary advances and trajectories. Tour. Manag. Perspect. **25**, 151 (2018)
45. J.K. Åstrøm, Why theming? Identifying the purposes of theming in tourism. J. Qual. Assur. Hosp. Tour. **21**(3), 245 (2020)
46. F. Cassia, P. Castellani, C. Rossato, C. Baccarani, Finding a way towards high-quality, accessible tourism: the role of digital ecosystems. TQM J. **33**(1), 205 (2021)
47. M. Shahzalal, I. Elgammal, Stakeholders' perception of accessible tourism implementation based on corporate sustainability and responsibility: a SEM-based investigation. Tour. Rev. 1 (2022)
48. D. Buhalis, S. Darcy, *Accessible Tourism: Concepts and Issues* (Channel View Publication, Bristol, 2011)
49. R. Singh, A. Ismail, S. PS, D. Singh, Compliance of accessibility in tourism websites: a pledge towards disability. J. Hospitality Tour. Insights **4**(3), 263 (2021)
50. M. Agovino, M. Casaccia, A. Garofalo, K. Marchesano, Tourism and disability in Italy. Limits and opportunities. Tour. Manag. Perspect. **23**, 58 (2017)
51. F. Magno, F. Cassia, Public administrators' engagement in services co-creation: factors that foster and hinder organisational learning about citizens. Total Qual. Manag. Bus. Excell. **26**(11–12), 1161 (2015)
52. A. Tlili, F. Altinay, Z. Altinay, Y. Zhang, Envisioning the future of technology integration for accessible hospitality and tourism. Int. J. Contemp. Hosp. Manag. **33**(12), 4460 (2021)
53. S. Darcy, B. Cameron, S. Pegg, Accessible tourism and sustainability: a discussion and case study. J. Sustain. Tour. **18**(4), 515 (2010)
54. P. Teixeira, L. Teixeira, C. Eusébio, S. Silva, A. Teixeira, in *ICT tools and applications for accessible tourism*. ed. by C. Eusébio, L. Teixeira, M.J. Carneiro (IGI Global, Hershey, PA, 2021), p.1

55. P. Accordino, R. Coppolino, E.T. La Rocca, in *Tourism and Disability: An Economic and Managerial Perspective*. ed. by T. Abbate, F. Cesaroni, A. D'Amico (Springer International Publishing, Cham, 2022), p.155
56. B. Casais, C. Castro, Online communication of accessibility conditions in touristic spots: The design–communication gap in Porto destination. J. Hosp. Tour. Technol. **12**(2), 196 (2021)

Chapter 4
Accessible Tourism from the Destination Perspective: Coordination Among Actors and Digital Ecosystems

Paola Castellani and Alfonso Vargas-Sánchez

Abstract Accessible tourism destinations provide both tourists and locals with substantial benefits, but the transition toward fully accessible tourism requires investment and appropriate governance mechanisms. This chapter discusses the role of technological and non-technological resources that enable a transition to accessible tourism and specifically addresses the relationship between accessible tourism and smart tourism destinations. The chapter also emphasizes the need for coordination among the multiple actors who belong to the destination's service ecosystem for successful accessible tourism, outlining both the formal and informal coordination mechanisms among actors. Finally, the specific contribution of digital ecosystems enabled by digital platforms is presented and discussed, highlighting that the establishment of digital platforms is necessary but not sufficient to establish effective digital collaboration among actors.

Keyword Accessible tourism · Smart tourism destination · Coopetition · Service ecosystems · Digital ecosystems · Destination management organization

4.1 The Value of Accessibility from the Destination Perspective: Quality and Reputation, Identity and Purpose

The term "accessible tourism" is relatively recent. According to Rubio-Escuderos et al. [1], it was first used in the academic literature in 1989, in a report by Baker titled "Tourism for all" [2]. Accessible tourism refers to the issue of accessibility

P. Castellani (✉)
University of Verona, Verona, Italy
e-mail: paola.castellani@univr.it

A. Vargas-Sánchez
University of Huelva, Huelva, Spain

F. Cassia et al. (eds.), *Accessible Tourism in the Digital Ecosystem*,
SpringerBriefs in Applied Sciences and Technology,
https://doi.org/10.1007/978-3-031-38782-1_4

through the removal of urban and architectural barriers as well as social integration through tourism for people with some kind of disability.

From the destination governance perspective, it is relevant to underline that:

- The segment of the population with some type of disability is becoming larger, in parallel to the general increase in life expectancy and demographic trends. In Europe, and around the world, there are millions of people with disabilities, as well as elderly individuals, with the need and purchasing power to enjoy tourist services. They have the right to enjoy leisure, life without barriers, and better training from the people who provide them with public and private services.
- The elimination of architectural and social barriers, as well as training in disability and accessibility, can also be a significant employment source due to the variety of occupations that arise in the provision of accessible tourism and leisure services.

Nonetheless, "accessibility does not only entail being a barrier-free destination, it also encompasses services that are multilingual and, for example, digitally available to all travellers or visitors—regardless of age, cultural background or any physical disability" [3, p. 7].

Despite the progress that has been made, Buj's [4, p. 16] statement regarding accessible tourism demand is still valid: "there is a demand for accessible tourism that is not met by the tourism sector and that truly accessible facilities, products and services are the exception rather than the rule. Unlike most products, the effort needs to be put into the product itself, rather than stimulating the demand."

It is worth emphasizing that:

- When a destination is accessible, both tourists and locals benefit from the corresponding improvements in accessibility to the urban environment, means of transport, and other kinds of services.
- The transition toward fully accessible tourism requires investment, the return of which would not just be a more inclusive and fair society but would also include economic returns for tourism businesses and destinations.

To guarantee that environments, goods, and services are globally accessible and can be enjoyed without difficulty or excessive effort, a set of requirements must be satisfied. These requirements are related to the actions of:

- Wandering (moving from one site to another, both horizontally and vertically),
- Apprehension (taking or grasping something),
- Location (finding out the precise place where something or someone is), and
- Communication (exchanging the information necessary for the development of an activity).

These requirements ensure that environments, goods, and services are adequate for the needs and expectations of all potential users, regardless of their age, sex, cultural origin, or degree of capacity.

The concept of accessibility is becoming increasingly present in all stages of the tourism value chain (accessible hotels, restaurants, beaches, museums, etc.), both for reasons of avoiding discrimination (not infringing on legally protected social rights) and the attractiveness of a growing market segment and its economic implications. These latter implications can be particularly significant in mature destinations, where accessibility can provide a competitive advantage over emerging destinations that may still be behind in this field. As Souca [5, p. 1155] stated, "to ignore its potential is to actually ignore fruitful business opportunities." This is true for several reasons: disabled individuals often become regular (loyal) clients after finding a tourism facility that suits their needs; they usually take longer holiday breaks than the average non-disabled individual; and they tend not to travel alone and to spend more money, especially in the off-season.

Consequently, it contributes to:

- Mitigating the seasonality of tourism. Many of the individuals benefiting from accessible tourism are inactive in the labor market, such as disability pensioners, and retirees, so they have time to travel throughout the year.
- Reinforcing the image (reputation) and competitiveness of the destination by differentiating the character of its connection with higher quality, socially responsible standards and embracing the most current concepts of smart tourist destinations (STDs).

In this respect, "accessibility also responds to an individual's right to open access to goods and services, it boosts de-seasonalisation, and improves the image of a destination, by positioning itself as socially responsible" [6, p. 45].

Although related, the concepts of tourist accessibility and accessible tourism must be differentiated. Tourist accessibility refers to the characteristics of a tourism service or facility that enable its use and enjoyment by anyone, regardless of his/her physical, sensory, mental, or cognitive capacity. Accessible tourism, on the other hand, refers to the activities of tourist establishments and companies in a destination that sell and promote universal accessibility and, therefore, are specifically aimed at a clientele of people with disabilities, together with family members and caregivers. The positioning of a tourism destination as accessible can only be achieved if a previous effort for real tourist accessibility has been made. This effort will not be fruitful without a participative and global (multi-stakeholder) approach to the construction of accessible destinations, "present throughout the entire tourism value chain" [6, p. 72], with the destination's actors working in an integrated way. As stated by Buj: "the transition to a more accessible tourism requires the involvement of all stakeholders, including tourism businesses and different levels of administration. The public sector has an essential role to play. Issues such as public financial support, certification, destination marketing and public infrastructure all require the involvement of every administrative level of political power (local, regional and national authorities as well as supranational)" [4, p. 52]. Buj elaborates further, stating: "separate and uncoordinated efforts alone will not make accessible tourism flourish. A holistic approach that covers transport, accommodation and attractions is indispensable to producing accessible destinations" [4, p. 55]. The idea of destinations as business ecosystems will be developed in the next section.

Smart tourist destinations combine the pillars of innovation, technology, sustainability, and universal accessibility, with the purpose of raising the quality of tourists' experiences and improving residents' quality of life (an example of a Smart Tourist Destination can be found at: https://www.segittur.es/en/smart-tourism-destinations/dti-projects/smart-destinations/). To constitute a genuine STD system, the pillars must be developed under the umbrella of mechanisms of tourism governance that are able to establish the core guidelines of destination identity/values and vision, shared by the actors involved [7]. The association with innovative technologies and the creation of an advanced digital space is insufficient if it is not a carrier of sustainability (in its various dimensions) and universal accessibility. Only an adequate combination of technological and non-technological (human and managerial) resources (hard and soft dimensions of intelligence, respectively) can bring about competitive advantages with the potential to be perpetually sustained.

Although currently a tourist destination can only be classified as smart if it has a good record on accessibility ("If it's not accessible, it's not smart" [6, p. 167]), this was not always the case. For example, Boes et al. [8] do not include this dimension in their conceptualization of an STD, although, conversely, for López de Ávila [9] one of the features of an STD is that it must be "accessible to everyone" (quoted by Gretzel et al. [10, p. 180]). It is important to clarify that its foundation is in contributing solutions—mainly based on the advances of information and communication technologies (ICTs)—that address issues of major importance including universal accessibility to destinations [11].

To make this possible at this point of the twenty-first century (in a truly global, digital, and hyper-connected industry), tourism governance needs to be revisited and revised into new forms [12]. The Spanish Norm UNE 178501:2018, on Requisites for Management System of Smart Destinations, is a pioneering standard [13] built on the above-mentioned pillars. The accessibility requisites for this certification include [13, pp. 38–39]:

- Show a documented commitment to improving the universal accessibility of the destination and ensuring compliance with the requirements in both public and private management.
- Dedicate means (human, technical, and financial) to the management of the destination's universal accessibility.
- Perform a documented diagnosis to determine the extent to which the requirements in the legislation on universal accessibility are met.
- Establish a plan of action for the improvement of universal accessibility.
- Agree on the scope of actions to be promoted in the universal accessibility plan with both public and private stakeholders.
- Establish participation mechanisms for stakeholders, including entities representing users.
- Ensure the training and competency in universal accessibility of the people who participate in the execution of the action plan (destination managers, professionals of the tourism sector in the public and private spheres, etc.).
- Provide information on universal accessibility services, as well as on the accessibility conditions of the destination's tourist offerings.
- Promote the accessible offering and facilitate its marketing.

- Undertake a follow-up of the plan of action on universal accessibility and a periodic evaluation of the fulfillment of its objectives and actions. Likewise, it must manage the incidents that may occasionally arise.
- Ensure compliance with universal accessibility measures established in the action plan.
- Work on the continuous improvement of universal accessibility in an integrated manner throughout the tourist offering, promoting awareness among stakeholders and compliance with current legislation and applicable voluntary reference regulations.

As pointed out by Vargas-Sánchez [11, p. 193]: "Tourism destination can be observed as a business ecosystem, with a higher and higher level of complexity—mainly because of the increasing interactions among its constituents and the consequent increasing difficulty to anticipate the outcomes of individual actions—which, in addition, is tried to be managed under the smartness perspective enabled by technology developments. As a result, a new lens is necessary. That proposed lens is the result of the integration of three originally isolated theoretical approaches: Business Ecosystem Theory, Complexity Theory and Smart Tourism" (an application of this lens to an industrial heritage destination can be found at [14]). The next sections of this chapter detail this ecosystemic approach and how it can impact the progress of tourist destinations' accessibility.

4.2 Destinations as Ecosystems of Actors at Different Levels

The term "business ecosystem" was first used by Moore [11, p. 194], who analyzes and defines the concept based on the analogy with the biological ecosystem, taking the theory of ecology as its foundation [15]. As business networks are characterized by a large number of loosely interconnected participants who depend on each other for their mutual effectiveness and survival [16], Moore [15] describes their co-evolution as the result of the complex interplay between competitive and cooperative business strategies.

This idea is easily transferable to a tourism destination, which can be viewed as a large, non-homogeneous set of actors (including providers of different kinds of services such as transport, accommodation, food, leisure activities, knowledge, technology, and digital solutions; intermediaries like tour operators, travel agencies; tourists; local communities; and governments), with different interests but interdependent for their mutual success, and, therefore, bound together in a collective whole [17]. Depending on the lens used, that collective whole can be observed at different levels—by city, region, country, or even globally—although the delimitation of the precise boundaries of a specific ecosystem can be fuzzy due to the interplay and interdependencies between the referred levels and the existence of multilevel players. In any case, "a tourism destination may be considered a network of public and private interrelated stakeholders" [14, p. 532], as well as the socioeconomic, institutional, and regulatory environments under which its various actors (buyers, producers, suppliers, both public and private) run their activities [18]. Its performance "as a whole depends on the web of connections between the various players, and not only on the intrinsic characteristics of the destination" [19, p. 170], which leads to the notion of tourism governance through collective actions (promotional ones, for instance) that favor the effective alignment of players toward common goals. The identification of collective interests, the establishment of links, and the coordination of negotiations are essential for the proper orchestration of tourism governance and, ultimately, destination success.

The business ecosystem theoretical framework connects with concepts such as collaboration (including coopetition), value co-creation, and co-evolution. Regarding co-evolution, any business ecosystem is considered to have its own life cycle, with four distinct stages of development: birth, expansion, leadership, and self-renewal [20]. This contribution preceded in the field of tourism with the Tourism Area Life Cycle (TALC) model for destinations, first appeared in the academic literature in 1980 [21], and was later enriched by the force field analysis (FFA) technique [22].

Both essential characteristics and organizing principles can be established for a business ecosystem. Essential characteristics include "inter-dependence of its components, cooperative evolution, simultaneous existence of competition and cooperation, the existence of numerous role players, dynamism and flexibility, shared fate, contribution to making innovations and achieving business successes," while the ideal organizing principles are interconnectedness, diversity, and complexity [23, p. 250].

It is worth noting that, according to Iansiti and Levien [17], a community will flourish only if its ecosystem is healthy, with three key elements contributing to that health: productivity, robustness, and niche creation, also known as efficiency, resilience, and the creation of meaningful diversity, respectively. The element of creating meaningful diversity should lead to target segments such as accessible tourism.

In this sense, Costa [24, p. 653] reports that "inclusive tourism promotes competitiveness by making the destination more accessible and so, able to receive any tourist," and, therefore the challenge of inclusion and accessibility facilitates the adaptation of policies to make destinations available for all, considering the impacts for destination branding. Costa et al. [25] propose an evolution toward a new model of tourism, designated as "positive tourism," that is able to add value to the tourism ecosystem when all tourist actors in a destination maintain their commitment to work together to promote universal accessibility and inclusiveness. As part of the current digital logic, they point out that a number of augmented reality-based solutions "can greatly help in aspects of tourism like inclusion, accessibility, safety, and tourism education" [25, p. 776].

4.3 The Need for Coordination Among the offering's Actors

Managing the development of tourism destinations is increasingly complex, especially in light of the many changes taking place. In this regard scholars point out: the overall growth of the tourism industry and competition, more experienced and demanding visitors, open discussion of the negative impacts of tourism, and various solutions for facing relevant emerging issues, including the actions and capabilities of many and new stakeholders across different domains (policies) and levels of governance [26, p. 213]. Tourism development requires embracing a multi-goal, multi-domain, multi-actor, and multilevel approach, as the interrelations and interdependencies of actors and their actions affect the attainment of individual and collective goals [27].

Tourist destinations are configured as complex networks in which many public, private, and third-party stakeholders coexist [28], occasionally interacting to create value for a wider tourism area. The involved players are committed to joining forces and capacities to conceive tourism products and experience design; accelerate innovations; engage in lobbying activities; and stimulate collective learning, business innovation, and placemaking [26, p. 214]. If actors can work together in the management of a destination in a strategic and well-organized way, providing for the division of tasks, roles, and responsibilities, they can give life to a cooperation system capable of creating value for all involved stakeholders. In this respect, informal arrangements and coordination mechanisms are important for the realization of value creation for the destination.

Few previous studies have focused on coordination mechanisms from an ecosystem perspective, involving a single actor, a specific business group, or independent and diverse public and private sector organizations. In particular, the difference in expectations between public and private sector organizations may require formal and informal coordination mechanisms, the latter of which can influence collaboration between heterogeneous organizations by balancing tensions that arise from cognitive elements [29].

Informal coordination mechanisms such as social ties, trust, and roles, and more formal coordination mechanisms such as plans and rules can effectively support the governance of cooperative interactions, mitigate tensions associated with coopetition, build a shared understanding, and help actors face the challenges of an ever-changing environment when managing joint activities. Informal and flexible mechanisms can be especially valuable as the number and types of relevant stakeholders in a destination continuously evolve and change over time.

As Mariani [30, p. 113] argued "roles (i.e., the role of a leading network or a coordinator) can provide vital elements for the relationship vision and for the needed flexibility to adapt to environmental changes; plans (such as schedules) can define and maintain the elements of the joint action while providing stability; trust can provide the opportunity to develop repeated relationships and strengthen relational benefits."

Overall, formal mechanisms tend to be reduced by and contracts replaced with relational skills and trust. Coordination mechanisms with varying degrees of formalization, such as social ties, trust, roles, plans, rules, and physical proximity, turn out to be more effective governance forms than contracts in determining how joint activities should be managed among networks [30, p. 113]. Specifically, the coordination mechanisms of trust, social ties, reciprocity, and roles play an important role in the formation and sustainability of coopetitive interactions. Other elements such as friendly relations among managers of destination management organizations (DMOs) facilitate the sharing of knowledge and information about strategic opportunities and operational issues both inside the destination and among destinations [31].

The following drivers are considered particularly important for formalizing the coordination mechanisms in inter-network coopetition: strong leadership; an effective brokerage and pivotal attitude; and a macro-focus on strategic thinking in a specific network [31]. Mariani's framework (2016) also underlines the importance of drivers such as power asymmetry; maturity of the network management approach; maturity and distance of the marketing approach; experience in working together; and cultural, functional, and organizational similarities. Each stage of the evolution of an inter-network coopetitive relationship has specific characteristics regarding the underlying coordination mechanisms [31].

The existing literature indicates that in the absence of coordination mechanisms, collaboration to bind connections is unsuccessful [32–34]. In particular, the ability to express extensive, efficient, and effective coordination among an offering's actors (i.e., deeply integrating partnerships' processes and systems) encourages growth in cooperation, possibly leading to a positive spiraling effect [35].

Coordination entities and mechanisms are tools for optimizing destinations' contributions and actively managing task inter-dependence. Social ties, trust, and roles are relevant for the success of a coopetitive inter-network relationship at each stage of the evolution, while plans and rules become significant in partnership selection and reinforcement.

4.4 The Coordination Modes Among an offering's Actors: The Contribution of Digital Ecosystems

There is no doubt that technology has progressed significantly and become more widely adopted among visitors over the decades, but the application of digital technology by DMOs to carry out their management role has been limited in general [36, 37].

As underlined by the literature, an important condition for the successful development and management of DMOs is effective collaboration among tourism stakeholders [37]. For example, empirical evidence demonstrates that digital collaboration is essential for micro-DMOs, who must transform their existing websites into digital platforms that act as a hub for business stakeholders' involvement [38]. Research commissioned by the UK government in 2021 surveyed over 280 tourism stakeholders and found that greater investment in digital technologies is needed to enable tourism stakeholders to collaborate and work more effectively [39, p. 5]. Digital technologies allow an offering's actors to match, connect, and communicate with less difficulty and continuously collect and share large volumes of information [40–42]. Digital collaboration for destination management is invaluable for the competitiveness of the destination [43].

Platform-based digital ecosystems allow each participant to share information, resources, and projects with all other participants which is very important given that destinations are complex ecosystems with many actors. In the offline world, exchanges are often mediated by a subject (e.g., a single DMO) that collects information and redistributes it; it is difficult, if not impossible, for an actor to communicate directly with all the other actors.

Tourism business stakeholders can better integrate into a digital ecosystem through the use of platforms [37]. The process of digital collaboration for destination management is strategic, defined as "the process whereby a group of autonomous stakeholders work toward achieving a common objective, using shared rules, norms and structures, facilitated by digital technologies" [38, p. 3]. Business stakeholders are able to collaborate directly on the digital platform for knowledge sharing, networking, and marketing. As digital platforms are transformed over time through incessant technological innovation, digital collaboration has a connotation of dynamism, and the tourism industry needs reliable technological structures that facilitate collaboration between its multiple players.

Studies confirm that similar elements underpin both digital collaboration and non-digital collaboration including trust, mutuality through collective benefit, control, and leadership [44, 45]. In digital collaboration, however, these elements have some specific attributes that require highlighting. Regarding the *trust* element (the most distinct aspect of digital collaboration compared to non-digital collaboration), Zainal-Abidin et al. [38, p. 10] point out that "trust is seen to be more complex and multilayered in digital collaboration. Besides trust toward the DMO and other organizations, an additional layer is trust toward the digital platform." In online contexts the channels of interaction are more limited than in face-to face contexts, so trust-building can be a relevant concern. Studies on the establishment and sustainment of trust on digital platforms in tourism are thus far limited. Trust can be supported through the sharing of organizational identity; a willingness to collaborate and set scopes; and an awareness of mutual needs and roles. It is also generated through a strong sense of behavior ethics between online collaborators and a trustworthy ICT promoting communication and reliability. Zainal-Abidin et al. [38] also highlight that digital collaboration can be successfully managed with a bottom-up approach and smart, effective destination *leadership* guiding flexible relationship structures. It is important to have not only a collaborative leader, but a leadership that is able to draw on other organizations to form collaborative communities. As underlined by Bahar et al. [46], a digital platform can facilitate organizational leaders in the optimization of network effects and community formation. Finally, as far as *control* (of security and functionality) is concerned, it is another key factor relating to shared data and the strategic use of data in developing new products [38]. The establishment of digital infrastructures is necessary but not sufficient for effective collaboration among a destination's actors. DMOs should take care to also foster non-technological factors that are necessary for digital collaboration, starting with enhancing trust among the actors.

References

1. L. Rubio-Escuderos, H. García-Andreu, J. Ullán de la Rosa, Eur. J. Tour. Res. **28**, 2803 (2021)
2. M. Baker, *Tourism for All: A Report of the Working Party Chaired by Mary Baker* (English Tourist Board in association with the Holiday Care Service, the Scottish Tourist Board, the Wales Tourist Board, London, UK, 1989)
3. Scholz & Friends Agenda Berlin GmbH, Compendium of Best Practices: *2019 European Capital of Smart Tourism competition* (European Commission, DG Growth Internal Market, Industry, Entrepreneurship and SMEs, 2019)
4. C. Buj, *Paving the Way to Accessible Tourism* (Leeds Metropolitan University, UK, International Centre for Responsible Tourism, 2010), p.77
5. M.L. Souca, University of Oradea. Ann. Fac. Econ. **1**, 2 (2010)
6. SEGITTUR, Smart Destinations Report: building the future (Secretary of State for Telecommunications & Secretary of State for Tourism, Madrid, Spain, 2015)
7. A. Vargas-Sánchez, Enlightening Tour. Pathmaking J. **6**, 2 (2016)
8. K. Boes, D. Buhalis, A. Inversini, in *Information and Communication Technologies in Tourism*, ed. by I. Tussyadiah, A. Inversini (Springer International Publishing Switzerland, 2015)
9. A. López de Ávila, Paper presented at the ENTER conference on information and communication technologies in tourism (Lugano, Switzerland, 2015)
10. U. Gretzel, M. Sigala, Z. Xiang, C Koo, Electron. Markets **25** (2015)
11. A. Vargas-Sánchez, Academic Papers presented at the 1st UNWTO world conference on smart destinations (UNWTO, Murcia, Spain, 2018)
12. A. Vargas-Sánchez, T. Abbate, M. Perano, in *Management and Sustainability: Creating Shared Value in the Digital Era—Proceedings of Sinergie-Sima Management Conference (Full Papers)*, ed. by A. Pastore, F. Testa, G. Iasevoli, M. Ugolini (Sapienza University of Rome, Rome, Italy, 2019)
13. AENOR, Sistema de Gestión de Destinos Turísticos Inteligentes: Requisitos (AENOR, Madrid, Spain, 2018)
14. M.C. Perfetto, A. Vargas-Sánchez, J. Herit. Tour. **13**, 6 (2018)
15. J.F. Moore, Harv. Bus. Rev. **71**, 3 (1993)
16. R. Lewin, *Complexity: Life at the Edge of Chaos* (University of Chicago, Chicago, 1999)
17. M. Iansiti, R. Levien, Harv. Bus. Rev. **82**, 3 (2004)
18. J.F. Moore, Wash. Q. **21**, 1 (1998)
19. W. Selen, R. Ogulin, Athens J. Tour. **2**, 3 (2015)
20. J.F. Moore, *The Death of Competition: Leadership and Strategy in the Age of Business* (Harper Collins Publisher, New York, 1996)
21. R.W. Butler, Can. Geogr. **24**, 1 (1980)
22. R.W. Butler, Tour. Recreat. Res. **34**, 3 (2009)
23. M.C. Perfetto, A. Vargas-Sánchez, A. Presenza, J. Spat. Organ. Dyn. **IV**, 3 (2016)
24. J. Costa, Worldwide Hospitality Tour. Themes **12**, 6 (2020)
25. J. Costa, M. Montenegro, J. Gomes, Worldwide Hospitality Tour. Themes **12**, 6 (2020)
26. S. Hartman, B. Wielenga, J.H. Heslinga, J. Tour. Futures **6**, 3 (2020)

27. S. Hartman, E. Innerholer, M. Fontanari, H. Pechlaner, *Destination and Opportunities for Destination Management and Governance* (Routledge, Abrington, 2018)
28. R. Baggio, M.M. Mariani, Anatolia Int. J. Tour. Hospitality Res. **23**, 1 (2012)
29. R. Lindgren, O. Eriksson, K. Lyytinen, J. Inf. Technol. **30**, 3 (2015)
30. M.M. Mariani, Ind. Market. Manag. **53** (2016)
31. A. Strobl, M. Peters, Ann. Tour. Res. **15**, 1 (2012)
32. D. Breslin, J. Kask, M. Schlaile, G. Abatecola, Ind. Market. Manag. **98** (2021)
33. S. Li-jin, C. Zhong, Adv. Soc. Sci. Educ. Human. Res. **176** (2018)
34. K. Möller, A. Rajala, Ind. Mark. Manage. **36**, 7 (2007)
35. R. Gulati, F. Wohlgezogen, P. Zhelyazkov, Acad. Manag. Ann. **6**, 1 (2012)
36. N. de Bois, *The de Bois Review: An independent review of Destination Management Organisations in England* (Department for Digital, Culture, Media & Sport United Kingdom, 2021)
37. J. Estêvão, M.J. Carneiro, L. Teixeira, J. Organ. Comput. Electron. Commer. **30**, 2 (2020)
38. H. Zainal-Abidin, C. Scarles, C. Lundberg, Tour. Manag. **96** (2023)
39. M. Llewellyn, *DMO Review Responses: Full Report* (Llewellyn McLaren Consulting, 2021).
40. A. Gawer, Innov. Organ. Manag. **24**, 1 (2021)
41. U. Gretzel, Eur. J. Tour. Res. **30**, 3002 (2022)
42. Y. Wang, L. Zhao, Requirements Eng. **24**, 2 (2019)
43. E. Sorokina, Y. Wang, A. Fyall, P. Lugosi, E. Torres, T. Jung, J. Destination Market. Manag. **23** (2022)
44. F. Zach, J. Hospitality Tour. Res. **40**, 3 (2016)
45. I. Önder, A. Berbekova, Int. J. Tour. Cities **8**, 3 (2022)
46. V.S. Bahar, S. Nenonen, R.G. Starr Jr., Tour. Manag. **88**, (2022)

Chapter 5
Accessible Tourism: Excellence Instances of Digital Ecosystem Logic in Place

Federico Brunetti, Paola Castellani, and Francesca Bazzani

Abstract To complete the book, this chapter presents two cases of working digital ecosystems. The first comes from Alto Adige, a well-known tourist region in the Italian Alps, while the second emerged in the UK, but works as a network all over the world. These cases serve as exemplars of the achievements a logic of IT-based cooperation can provide, highlighting the power of working together on the one hand, and of the digital tools on the other. Thanks to the opportunities provided by such networks, tourism for people with disability is becoming more accessible, paving the way, hopefully, for the very removal of the word 'accessible'.

Keywords Accessible tourism · Case studies · Accessible tourism projects

5.1 Introduction to the Analysis of Real-World Experiences: Methodological Issues

Publishing a book on accessible tourism without any empirical elements would not be well-conceived. Even from a theoretical perspective, real-world examples are useful, because, ultimately, accessible tourism is a practical concern, something that requires support not only in terms of conceptual clarification but from real-world experiences. Accessible tourism is important particularly because, when combined with friends and family, the disability market affects about 70% of tourists/consumers [1, p. 9].

However, the academic literature on accessible tourism is still in its infancy; published papers dealing with this topic are few, and even fewer include actual and specific instances of accessible tourism in practice. Thus, good case studies of accessible tourism are highly needed, because, when it comes to introducing any change, working examples play a fundamental role, first as a trigger, to prove that change is possible, and second, to pave the way towards broader transformation.

F. Brunetti · P. Castellani (✉) · F. Bazzani
University of Verona, Verona, Italy
e-mail: paola.castellani@univr.it

F. Cassia et al. (eds.), *Accessible Tourism in the Digital Ecosystem*, SpringerBriefs in Applied Sciences and Technology,
https://doi.org/10.1007/978-3-031-38782-1_5

An empirical point of view may imply either a quantitative or qualitative approach. A quantitative approach—collecting data on the number of tourists with disabilities, their arrivals and presence at different facilities or destinations, the number of facilities or destinations suitable to host disabled tourists and so on—is certainly useful, but at the end of the day, lacks meaning. Of more interest—at least in our opinion—is to assess real examples that can provide empirical support for the ideas developed in this volume. Real examples, though just a 'cherry-picked' selection of the whole of reality, provide a more vivid representation of what accessible tourism in practice can mean and, incidentally, offer greater inspiration than numbers and statistics.

To this end, a qualitative approach—namely, a case-study approach—is followed in this chapter. As always, this choice comes with advantages and disadvantages but, as has been previously noted, the actual experiences of organisations bring a greater contribution to the understanding and, possibly, to the managing and improving of accessible tourism.

One key issue to naturally arise concerns the choice of what experience to present. This is not an easy or obvious choice since there are many good practices regarding accessible tourism with respect to different kinds of disability, destinations and facilities. Many cities, hotels, museums, spas and amusement parks, for example, offer experiences inclusive of every type of tourist. These tend to be well known by the people who, for one reason or another, are in need of such inclusivity but not known at all, or little, by the general public—and often also by experts. To our minds, each and every of these deserves interest and appreciation, because they provide useful services, but often not adequately understood, demonstrating a meritorious sense of inclusion, participation and care-giving. But, of course, a selection had to be made, and we defined two criteria to aid with this: consistency with the approach of this volume and relevance in terms of good practice.

In line with the first criterion, we searched for cases where a digital ecosystem was involved; that is, a logic of technology-supported cooperation among different suppliers. According to the second criterion, we searched for cases that provided a good degree of effectiveness in dealing with tourism accessibility issues. Our search resulted in two cases: *Alto Adige per Tutti* and *Hidden Disabilities Sunflower*. Both of these comprise a network of interconnected actors based on an IT-enabled platform and both provide effective solutions to make it possible for tourists with disabilities to travel with a certain degree of ease.

As will hopefully become clear in the following pages, *Alto Adige per Tutti* and *Hidden Disabilities Sunflower* exhibit both originality and exemplarity. They serve as examples of digital ecosystems in action on the one hand and act as reference experiences to emulate or be inspired from on the other.

Needless to say, our hope is that accessible tourism, both as a concept and as a practice, will no longer have reason to exist in the near future. Every tourist destination, every tourist accommodation, means of transportation, attraction and so on is expected to become accessible to everyone. Designing an inclusive experience creates benefits for the whole system.

Accessibility as a feature of the tourism industry should fade, because, by definition, tourism is an escape from daily routine, leisure and entertainment, and these needs are even more important for those who live in a condition of diversity—whatever it may be.

Along this path, instances such as *Alto Adige per Tutti* and *Hidden Disabilities Sunflower* act as fundamental milestones to make it possible—and indeed, easy—for people with disability to live away from home as smoothly as everybody else.

5.2 Case History: The Accessible Tourism Project *Alto Adige Per Tutti*—South Tyrol for All

According to the World Health Organization (WHO), as of 2021, an estimated 1.3 billion people (16% of the global population) experience significant disability. This number is growing, driven by the increase in the number of people with non-communicable diseases, who are living longer and ageing with limitations in functioning [2, p. 15]. In Europe, people with disability (PWD) number 87 million (https://www.consilium.europa.eu/en/infographics/disability-eu-facts-figures/). In Italy, according to Istat data from 2019, PWD—or those who suffer from health problems or serious limitations that prevent them from carrying out their usual activities—numbered some 3.15 million (5.2% of the population). The elderly population is the most affected: almost 1.5 million people over 75 (22% of the population in that age group) live with disability, with 1 million of these women. The regions in which the phenomenon is most widespread are Umbria and Sardegna (6.9% and 7.9% of the population, respectively), while Lombardia and Trentino Alto Adige have the lowest prevalence (4.1% and 3.8%, respectively) [3, p. 11].

In the Trentino Alto Adige region (composed of the two autonomous areas Trentino and Alto Adige), tourism is a fundamental driver of the local economy and various innovative development projects are aimed at making the area accessible to people with physical, sensory and intellectual disabilities. The region is located in northern Italy and offers mountain tourism, both in winter and in summer. As expressed by the tour operator *Trentino Holidays*, 'We need to work on all aspects of the offer with the criterion of continuous improvement of universal accessibility, promoting inclusive marketing, transparent and reliable information, a mapping of tour operators sensitive to the issue of accessibility, of cultural and architectural barriers and transport enabling independent travel' (https://www.ildolomiti.it/cronaca/2022/il-38-delle-persone-in-trentino-alto-adige-e-disabile-e-il-52-in-italia-si-lavora-al-turismo-accessibile-unopportunita-commerciale-per-le-destinazioni-e-imprese). All efforts are focused on enabling the Trentino Alto Adige region to become an inclusive tourist destination, recognised by the target audience as reliable, organised and a truly excellent Italian destination (https://www.ildolomiti.it/politica/2022/il-turismo-accessibile-e-aperto-a-tutti-non-significa-solo-strutture-ad-hoc-per-persone-disabili-la-ministra-stefani-la-creazione-di-un-fondo-idea-nata-in-trentino). As highlighted by scholars, the two main principles for community values, culture and social progress are sustainability and accessibility [4, 5]. Guaranteeing

Alto Adige
per tutti
TURISMO ACCESSIBILE

Fig. 5.1 Alto Adige per Tutti logo

accessibility for all to tourism facilities, products and services should be a central part of any responsible and sustainable tourism policy. Accessibility is not only about human rights; it is a business opportunity for destinations and companies to embrace all visitors and enhance their revenues (https://www.unwto.org/accessibility).

In this regard, attention is drawn to the *Alto Adige per Tutti* project (Fig. 5.1), whose mission is to make tourism in Alto Adige-South Tyrol accessible to everyone, as everyone has the right to enjoy the beauty of nature and the marvellous panoramas of the region without obstacle. Families travelling with strollers, people in wheelchairs or people with mobility difficulties often have to give up on rough terrain destinations, where rocky paths, climbs or high mountain walls can form insurmountable barriers.

A commitment towards a tourism for all does not create special offers for people considered 'different' but enhances and optimises already existing features by making them known, for the benefit of the elderly or fragile and families with children, whether they are tourists or residents. Tourism for all looks at the 'person' and their interests, the desire for discovery and to have fun at any age and regardless of physical condition (https://www.turismosenzabarriere.it/turismo_disabilita.html).

The *Alto Adige per Tutti* project was powered by the *social co-operative independent L. onlus*, founded in 1997 on the initiative of nine people in wheelchairs 'to promote independent living, that is to offer disabled people stimuli and motivation to lead an independent life. To conceive, propose and develop tools to help achieve social integration. To be a consultancy and information centre for PWD by providing knowledge, technologies, professionalism and experience in the interest of society and in full respect of everyone's rights' (https://www.independent.it/it/cooperativa-independent).

Since 1999, independent L. has been a member of the European Network on Independent Living (ENIL), a PWD organisation founded in 1989 in Strasbourg that works to disseminate and promote the application of definitions, concepts and principles of independent life (https://www.independent.it/it/studi-ricerche). The projects and studies of the non-profit organisation Independent L. are aimed at the social inclusion of PWD and the promotion of their greatest possible in almost all areas of life (including private and professional life and education), using technologies at the forefront.

The non-profit organisation independent L., through a multidisciplinary and highly specialised team, provides integrated personalised consultancy services to individuals, social and health advisors, companies, schools and other public institutions. It is also recognised as a training provider and offers qualification courses in information technologies and administration aimed at the employment of PWD, supported by the European Social Fund, the Ministries of Labour, Health, Social Affairs in Italy and the Autonomous Province of Bolzano-South Tyrol (Italy). Innovative projects (many recognised as best practice by the European Union), scientific research and publications contribute to improving, over time, independent L.'s know-how and skills, with the benefits of such knowledge spread to the wider public (https://www.smart-museums.eu/en/partner).

Specialist advisory services include the areas of barrier-free access and inclusive tourism. In this regard, since 2004, the independent L. team has successfully managed the accessible tourism portal *Alto Adige per Tutti*. The institutional websites developed by the cooperative have given the in-house 'Webcenter' (main area of employment in the cooperative) recognition in 2017 by Agenzia per l'Italia Digitale (AgID) as one of the four national digital accessibility assessment centres (https://www.smart-museums.eu/en/partner).

Following this, independent L. has been engaged in the promotion of accessible tourism in the Alpine and pre-Alpine World Heritage Areas in partnership with two important cross-border projects: Interreg V-A Italy-Austria project 'Granting Accessible Tourism for Everyone (2017–2020)', which involves the use of new technologies, in collaboration with the Foundation Unesco Dolomites (Project Leader) (https://www.independent.it/it/progetto-gate); and Interreg V-A Italy-Austria project 'Small Museums Alliance Representing Territories (2019–2022)' to promote a culture of accessibility among tourism-cultural operators and the active participation of citizens in the enhancement of local natural and cultural heritage as a common good (https://www.smart-museums.eu/).

In the tourism destination of Alto Adige, one of the relevant best practices (due to the shared values of all stakeholders involved) is the accessible tourism supported by the tourism portal *Alto Adige per Tutti*, which enables a well-functioning digital ecosystem. It provides reliable information in the Italian and German languages about accessible destinations, hotels, restaurants, sights and attractions as well as information regarding accessibility of leisure attractions and public transport. Moreover, an English version is planned to follow as soon as possible.

From the offering side, technology is increasingly enabling tourism companies and the other actors in the tourism value ecosystem to support more effective tourism experiences [6].

This portal *Alto Adige per Tutti* was created by the independent L. team to offer all guests a 'carefree' stay without barriers in Alto Adige-South Tyrol. It is an innovative good practice that stands out for several reasons:

- It was conceived, designed and developed by the independent L. team itself.
- It detects tourist facilities according to their accessibility and proposes itineraries for PWD (https://www.suedtirol.info/it)
- It aims to be functional, especially for PWD, elderly people and families with children.
- It is designed for a good user experience: affordance, mapping and constraints are mainstream features of the website. High profiling of data and photographs on the accessibility characteristics of hotels, restaurants, museums, swimming pools,

cable cars, trains and walks, verified directly by the independent L. team, allow tourists to independently manage their experience.
- The data update process is continuous and rigorous.

In the development of accessible tourist destinations, the engagement of PWD and PWD organisations in the process enables these groups to participate in strategic decision-making, as well as in the conception, design, development and delivery of services (tourism and other). It is essential to involve PWD when deciding on the interventions to be included in benefit packages of care for universal health coverage and when designing plans for health emergencies. Bringing diversity, experience, expertise and knowledge, PWD can and should influence how policies and services are designed, commissioned and delivered; they can also reveal inequities on the ground that would otherwise be unknown to health policymakers [7].

In 2013, an *Alto Adige per Tutti* application (iPhone and Android) was produced, to match the different digital generation needs. Detailed information on over 600 accessible structures divided into thematic areas (accommodation, eating, strolling, discovering, moving around) is channelled into the application, which can be downloaded free of charge from iTunes and Google Play, and is available to tourists and citizens with special needs such as disabled, infirm or elderly people, but also families with small children. At the same time, the *Alto Adige per Tutti* website (Fig. 5.2) has been restyled and refreshed keeping in mind the latest advice on digital accessibility (https://www.independent.it/it/studi-ricerche).

In 2015, *Alto Adige per Tutti* joined the European Network for Accessible Tourism, and in 2016, the project was strengthened with the design and implementation of the free *Finding Parking* application which, in a simple and intuitive manner, provides directions to reach the parking spaces reserved for PWD present throughout the province. It also offers the possibility of reporting new car parks, commenting on existing ones or notifying other users of any access difficulties (https://www.suedtirol.info/it/informazioni/app-alto-adige/trova-parcheggi). As the portal clarifies, the project envisaged the geo-referenced detection of reserved parking spaces across the 116 Municipalities of South Tyrol—from the data therein, it appears that the general condition of 1317 parking spaces are satisfactory; 45% of the parking spaces are compliant with the law (in a suitable place, with flooring that facilitates movement for a person in a wheelchair and signage in accordance with the law) while the remaining 55% may cause difficulties due to incorrect configuration or careless choice of location.

- *A multidisciplinary network*

The *Alto Adige per Tutti* portal is supported by the Autonomous Province of Bolzano—Alto Adige and the Cassa di Risparmio di Bolzano Foundation. It also benefits from the recognition of public institutions such as the National Tourism Agency (Italy) and the European Network for Accessible Tourism.

There are around 600 structures that can be reached through the portal, all personally tested by the independent L. team, which over time has built a database capable

Fig. 5.2 Alto Adige per Tutti—experience page

of communicating 'real on-the-ground conditions' of the offer and the level of accessibility of the tourism structures in the region.

The portal provides users with a wealth of information, photographs and detailed descriptions of various hospitality facilities such as hotels, wellness hotels, apartments, hostels, campsites and other options, places to eat such as restaurants, pizzerias, bars, huts, mountain huts, ice cream shops, pastry shops, bistros, cultural places such as museums and tourist attractions, and sporting activities that can be enjoyed in South Tyrol. In addition, shopping centres, parking areas, amusement areas such as playgrounds, rides and swimming pools with waterslides for family holidays with children are also listed. Another significant topic addressed is barrier-free mobility via railways, ski lifts and nature walks.

The *Alto Adige per Tutti* network is multidisciplinary, involves experts from different backgrounds and includes persons with disabilities. It is important to promote and strengthen actions to secure the rights and the services necessary for persons with disabilities, thus facilitating their employment and a quality of life equal to that of others in the community [2, p. 174].

The network is supported by actors that aim to avoid a fragmented voice for the accessible tourist offer of the region and address the challenges they face as part of the same tourism destination [8, p. 214]. This can guarantee opportunities for cross-learning and knowledge-sharing among partners to drive timely and concrete actions for disability inclusion and accessible tourism [2, p. 175].

Specific characteristics of the accessible tourism portal Alto Adige per Tutti

Among the characteristics that distinguish the *Alto Adige per Tutti* platform is its creation by PWD, who have first-hand experience and understanding of the difficulties and needs of the community.

The profiling of data on accessibility and spaces of the host structures is high, though information on nutrition is more limited.

The structures reported by the portal have been tested by the independent L. team, strengthening the reliability of the information provided on the accessibility of individual companies (Figs. 5.3, 5.4 and 5.5).

- *Benefits for users and for businesses involved in accessible tourism*

The establishment of a digital ecosystem aims to make the territory an inclusive, warm and welcoming location where people want to live or stay. Hence, by providing

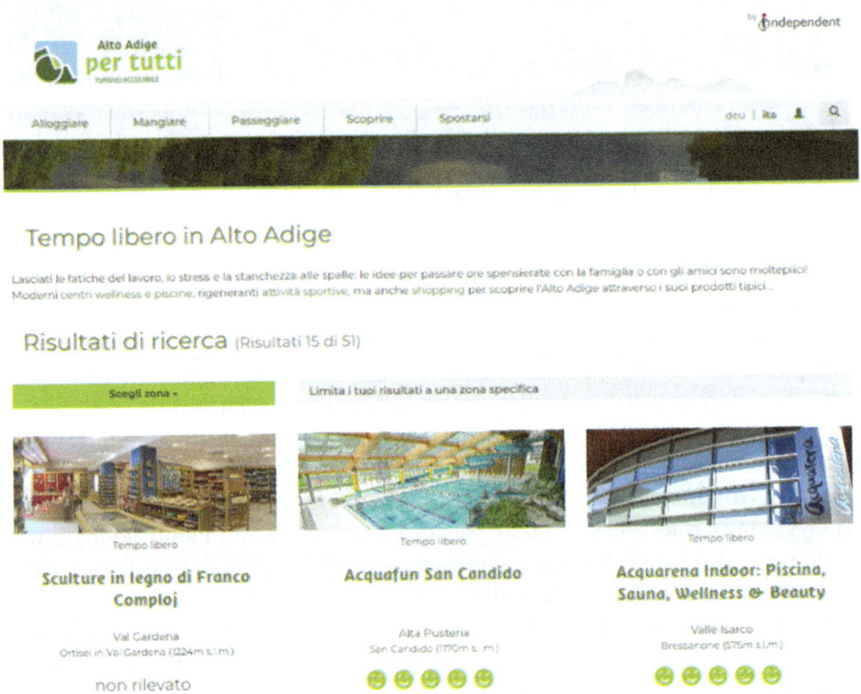

Fig. 5.3 Alto Adige per Tutti—experience results

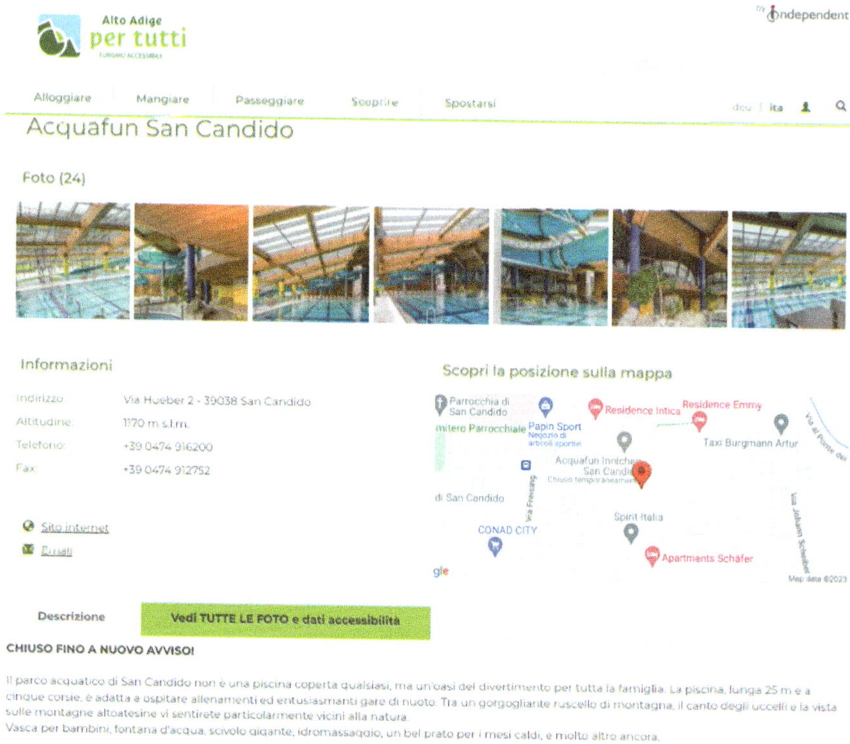

Fig. 5.4 Alto Adige per Tutti—experience company profile

an engagement platform, technology can act as an operant resource, disrupting the myopia guiding each actor's individual behaviours [9, p. 217].

Technology should be conceived as an operant resource able to bring about changes in ecosystems and influence value co-creation processes. The provision of a platform to support the engagement of actors involved in accessible tourism can represent an important step to first removing informational and relational barriers, and over time, smoothening other barriers (e.g. cultural barriers) [9, p. 216].

Users can take advantage of a clear portal and real utility given the availability of tested and measured information on the accessibility of the structures involved in the tourist offer of the destination. Through the site, people can access an application that allows them to easily identify accessible reserved parking spaces, an important service to facilitate the mobility of all tourists.

The *Alto Adige per Tutti* portal is highly specialised, among the few available in Italy. It provides support to the perception of the brand of the mapped structures and offers a trustworthy service to a faithful market niche. It is a 'good practice' that improves the propensity to listen and plan experiences aimed at people's real needs. It therefore contributes to the diffusion of wellbeing and strengthens the sharing

Fig. 5.5 Alto Adige per Tutti—experience company accessible detailed information

of the values of inclusion and equal opportunities in local communities and in the development of relationships between them and the tourists with whom they interact.

- *Future challenges and commitments for* Alto Adige per Tutti

There are various future challenges that the *Alto Adige per Tutti* platform could aim to pursue. Among these, we believe that the creation of a community and its involvement in animating social networks is important. In this regard, the efficient management of an Instagram and YouTube page could make it possible to further enhance the communication of the *Alto Adige per Tutti* project.

The visibility of the platform at an international level and the accessibility of its information could be further enhanced by introducing communication in English and creating an application for smartphones.

Another challenge concerns the expansion of the territory, involving further actors in the supply system committed to supporting the accessible development of the region.

The high scalability of the format managed by *Alto Adige per Tutti* requires a growing commitment to training for the profiling team. Furthermore, the format has the characteristic of being replicable in other destinations where detailed profiling on the accessibility of the structures in the tourist offer system is still lacking or limited.

One aspect of the analysed model that could be improved concerns the profiling of food, since the information currently available is limited to no gluten without indications of any AIC (Italian Celiac Association) certifications or other.

We believe that it could also be useful to create a standardised and unified network, which local communities could manage to better profile their destination.

5.3 Case History: *Hidden Disability Sunflower*—A Discreet Way to Make the Invisible Visible

The following case history has been selected due its relevance to non-visible disabilities, also known as invisible or hidden disabilities. Although the International Symbol of Accessibility (ISA), created in 1969 by the global organisation Rehabilitation International (https://www.riglobal.org/about), represents a familiar image of a person in a wheelchair, many disabilities are non-visible at first glance. The latest *Global Report on Health Equity for Persons with Disabilities* estimates that, in 2021, approximately 1.3 billion people—about 16% of the global population—experienced disability [2, p. 15], with about 71% of those non-visible, including learning, cognitive or neurological disability [1, p. 13], to name but a few.

Business has yet to discover disability as an emerging market [10, p. 13], however, the disability market potentially controls over 13 trillion dollars in disposable income [1, p. 1]. Although this figure underlines great opportunities, daily experience surveys suggest a very low customer satisfaction rate: when asked, PWD describe about 75–80% of their customer experiences as failures [1, p. 13].

If in all customer-centred business, the continuous pursuit of customer satisfaction leads all projects to create, increase and share values in the company and among stakeholders, from this perspective, the primary need is to shift the disability paradigm from 'added cost and effort' to 'added value' by demonstrating the shareholder value of disability [11, p. 4]. Shifting the consideration of disability from 'an exception' to part of the broader consumer and talent marketplace means moving to a new concept of designing experiences where 'delight for every person' is the goal and 'accessible' is an outcome of success [1, p. 16]. Invisible disabilities represent a great challenge for experience designers due to the high variability of individual situations and the difficulties in recognising these at first glance.

Hidden Disability Sunflower (Fig. 5.6), part of Hidden Disabilities Sunflower Scheme Limited, a private company based in the UK, is a working method conceived in 2016 '*to enable people with non-visible disabilities to access the support they need. It acts as a prompt for someone to choose to let people around them know they have a non-visible disability and that they may need a helping hand, understanding, or simply more time*' (https://hiddendisabilitiesstore.com/).

Hidden Disability Sunflower was chosen as a case study for the following reasons:

Fig. 5.6 Hidden disabilities sunflower logo

- It has a global reach and specialises in hidden disabilities: created in the UK in 2016, within a few years, it has become global and spread to different industries (https://hiddendisabilitiesstore.com/).
- It keeps in consideration both tangible elements and the intangible and emotional elements of each relationship, such as sensibility, respect, discretion and acceptance.
- It helps to create and spread a new positive diversity and inclusion culture. This is captured in the Sunflower as a symbol of openness and acceptance towards all diversities, with positive outcomes in the workplace and in society more widely (https://hiddendisabilitiesstore.com) [12].
- It supports companies to create standard working routines, to teach and train employees to define a replicable level of quality everywhere and for everyone.
- Innovation: it is not only a scheme of accessibility but also improves the total service experience connected to the ecosystem. Insights and innovation derived from disability improve the experience for all [1, p. 16].

A PWD may join *Hidden Disability Sunflower* by simply wearing a Sunflower lanyard (Fig. 5.7) in places where the scheme is recognised. The lanyard can be integrated with a card containing personal data, type of disability and a short explanation of support needed.

The lanyard is a code that discreetly indicates to people around the wearer including staff, colleagues and health professionals that the wearer needs additional support, help or a little more time (Figs. 5.8 and 5.9). However, this is only scratching the surface of this complex and innovative working method. It all started in 2016 at

Fig. 5.7 Hidden disabilities sunflower lanyard

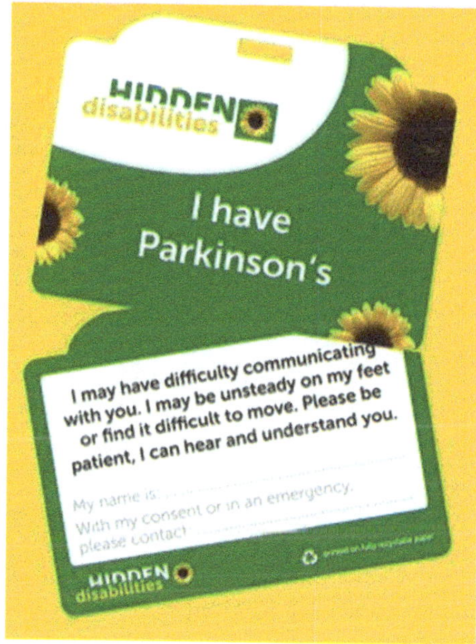

Fig. 5.8 Hidden disabilities sunflower Parkinson's card example

Gatwick Airport, where the accessibility team asked itself how they could recognise, among 500,000 passengers per year, persons with hidden disabilities (https://hiddendisabilitiesstore.com/insights/post/the-hidden-disabilities-sunflower-history). In addition to this main question, they also formulated rules to be respected as to how to create standard operations and how to train employees.

Hidden Disability Sunflower has developed a business model based on six basic pillars: membership, knowledge, training, working routine, marketing and community (Fig. 5.10).

With membership to the scheme, companies and charities benefit from the functionality of a Sunflower account, including training, member discounts, tailored inspiration and communication and inclusion tips to support their diversity and equity objectives. Sunflower members may add their Sunflower-friendly credentials onto a Sunflower locator map, so they can be found by PWD (https://hiddendisabilitiesstore.com/sunflower-memberships).

The Sunflower lanyard has achieved rapid success—as of 2021, the scheme has been adopted across a wide range of sectors in the UK, including retail, travel, tourism, schools, colleges, over 450 universities, airlines, airports, railway network, leisure facilities, cinemas (https://www.alzheimers.org.uk/blog/what-makes-dementia-friendly-cinema), healthcare and financial services. Members are continuously increasing, and coverage now includes the Americas, Europe, Oceania and the Middle East.

The success of the Sunflower lanyard can also be explained by its fast increase in social media followers, who share initiatives, goals and positive case histories

Fig. 5.9 Hidden disabilities sunflower Dyslexia card text example

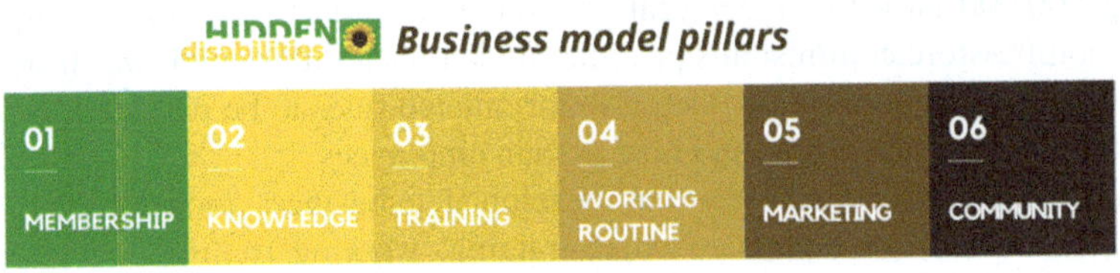

Fig. 5.10 Hidden disabilities sunflower business model pillars

and experiences (https://hiddendisabilitiesstore.com/insights/post/the-hidden-disabilities-sunflower-history).

Several stakeholders were involved in the early stages. Some were inside the airport environment such as the Airport Passenger Advisory Group, but it was acknowledged that the scheme required local and national charities' assessment on the real support for PWD and match their needs, and technical partners to organise wide staff training. At the first assessment, these included Alzheimer's Society UK, UK National Autistic Society and Visualise, a consultant and training company specialising in accessibility, inclusion and equity.

The website was designed around a blend of tangible and intangible elements: the desire to create an international symbol, recognised by everyone and everywhere, of care and inclusion; a global community of companies who share the same inclusive and innovative culture and values, and who co-create new cultural, societal and sustainable values; standardisation of training and working routines that make life easier and more comfortable for PWD; and a global marketing and communication plan to inspire societal cultural change.

From a digital perspective, *Sunflower Hidden Disabilities* is a wide and complex platform that includes many different functions, including where to find information about a project, how to become a member, membership area by login and password, an online shop, general information, FAQ areas, news and insights about disability. Although complex, it is well-designed by affordance, mapping and constraints elements. Digital accessibility is retained via constant updates and refreshing of the website (https://hiddendisabilitiesstore.com/accessibility). In its starting project and continuous development, *Sunflower Hidden Disabilities* embodies a digital ecosystem logic and scheme that ensure benefits for all stakeholders involved.

Wearing the Sunflower lanyard provides a sense of great relief and acceptance, reducing the level of friction while seeking service, such as anxiety, exclusion or having to make inappropriate or unpleasant explanations to staff and the public; with few words, it offers a seamless and effortless experience. As Kerry, a mother of two kids with disability living on Jersey (Channel Isles), said, '*Shopping is quite an issue for a parent like me, so to have a shop which is aware of hidden disabilities, most places are not, was such a great relief for us, as a family. [...] It helped massively. We were able to come shopping with the peace of mind, that it's ok if we have a meltdown during the trip*' (https://youtu.be/OzuRrKql3vs).

For a company, charity or sole trader, becoming a Sunflower Business Member means, for a yearly fee, benefitting from Sunflower training, knowledge and experience, tailored inspiration and communication and inclusion tips to support the member's diversity and equity objectives. There are also member discounts for buying lanyards and other communication products. While there is a long list of practical advantages of becoming a business partner, from an intrinsic value perspective, the main benefit is the possibility to make a positive change in the business and the societal environment.

Ryanair, known in the airline business as providing low-fare flight services (https://mission-statement.com/ryanair/), joined the Sunflower scheme in October 2022. As Tristan Casson-Rennie, Regional Director, Ireland & Northern Ireland for *Hidden Disabilities Sunflower*, said, '*We are delighted that Ryanair, the largest European airline by scheduled passengers, has joined the global Hidden Disabilities Sunflower network. Passengers with non visible disabilities can fly to 36 countries knowing that they will be supported by Ryanair crew in 228 airports. Travel is becoming more accessible for people who are disabled, extending the opportunities for exploration, work and play. Sunflower wearers will be met with kindness, patience and understanding by the Ryanair team from check-in to the end of their flight*' (https://corporate.ryanair.com/news/ryanair-becomes-first-irish-airline-to-launch-hidden-disabilities-sunflower/)

Looking at the *Sunflower Hidden Disabilities* scheme suggests several features that make it an innovative and interesting case/champion to be considered 'best practice' for accessibility:

- The airport starting point was a challenge due to its complex reality, but also offered great support because it is already structured by international strict procedures and workflows.
- It offers a scalable and replicable business model with affordable adjustments for sectors and cultural differences.
- Its economically sustainable business model supported by revenues (yearly membership fees, sales of lanyard and gadgets) free *Hidden Disabilities Sunflower* from public and private funding that may potentially influence corporate strategies and decision-making processes.
- Revenue performance: including insights from the disability market, companies enhance the customer experiences for PWD and their family and friends. In general, the design of solving pain points facing extreme users also improves usability for the average user [1, p. 26].
- Digital rationalisation: creation of videos to optimise information and standard training for members to conserve energy to concentrate on customised advisory services.
- It focuses on a lively yet unsatisfied market: the invisible disabilities market has a high rate of failed customer experiences [1, p. 13], and need and deserve to be 'delighted'. A barrier-free hotel (physical building) is a basic component of a good overnight stay for PWD, but this could be boosted to a welcoming relationship and an experience designed around people's needs.
- Creation of strong personal bond: through fragility and emotions recognition. The wearing of a lanyard is not limited to those with diagnoses/certification of disability; people who are temporarily in a condition of fragility or waiting for a diagnosis can also request a lanyard, to provide support during this sensitive period where emotions are more acute than usual.
- Community bond and network among stakeholders: this enhances the co-creation of sustainable and inclusive values at economic, societal and cultural levels.
- An ever-growing community due to an open search for new affiliates.

Final Remark

Following our study, we consider that *Hidden Disabilities Sunflower* could address the following future challenge:

- Development of experiential training projects: a next step could be the creation of training and education via augmented reality (AG) or virtual reality (VR). Virtual reality, augmented reality and mixed reality have been used for years in the education sector, from primary to university. There are several benefits to such use, from increasing employee motivation and engagement to improving performance and encouraging greater critical thinking [13, p. 223]—effects that are positive in the long term for all stakeholders.

References

1. R. Donovan, *Desigh Delight from Disability. 2020 Annual Report: The Global Economics of Disability* (The Return on Disability Group, September 1, 2020)
2. World Health Organization, *Global Report on Health Equity for Persons with Disabilities* (2022)
3. Istat, Audizione dell'Istat presso il Comitato Tecnico Scientifico dell'Osservatorio Nazionale sulla condizione delle persone con disabilità (24 marzo, 2021, https://www.istat.it/it/files/2021/03/Istat-Audizione-Osservatorio-Disabilit%C3%A0_24-marzo-2021.pdf)
4. A. Laaksonen, *Making Culture Accessible* (Council of Europe, Strasbourg, 2010)
5. T. Hancock, Health Promot. Int. **16**, 275 (2001)
6. T. Pencarelli, Inf. Technol. Tourism **1** (2019)
7. World Health Organization, WHO global strategy on people-centred and integrated health services: interim report (World Health Organization, 2015). https://apps.who.int/iris/handle/10665/155002
8. S. Hartman, B. Wielenga, J. Hessel Heslinga, J. Tourism Futures **6**, 213 (2020)
9. F. Cassia, P. Castellani, C. Rossato, C. Baccarani, TQM J. **33**, 205 (2021)
10. The Return on Disability® Company, Toronto, 3rd April 2013, *Sustainable Value Creation Through Disability*
11. The Return on Disability® Group, Toronto, *Revenue Drives Value in Disability Markets—Factor Analysis* (2015)
12. S.P. Tiwari, Technium Soc. Sci. J. **30**, 159 (2022)
13. A. Hanlon, *Digital Marketing* (Sage Publications, 2022)

Chapter 6
Conclusion. Accessible Tourism, Make It Happen!

Claudio Baccarani and Daniela Cavallo

Abstract The concept itself of tourism carries the ethical value of making the travel experience possible for every person who wishes to live it, regardless of the potential fragility or inconvenience they may feel. Significant advancements are being made toward the goal of accessible tourism, and digital platforms are supporting this process. However, the purpose of genuinely accessible tourism from a perspective of equal dignity of people cannot be achieved without a collective disposition toward welcoming by all the tourism operators, local authorities, and the resident population of tourist destinations. Hence, this section introduces and discusses the importance of welcoming to achieve accessible tourism.

Keywords Accessible tourism · Accessibility · Welcoming · Tourism destinations

The term "tourism" comes from the French word *tourisme*, which in turn refers to the French word *tour*, meaning "journey." In its prevailing meaning, tourism encompasses "the set of multipurpose activities and services that refer to the temporary transfer of people from their habitual residence to another location for a certain purpose" (Treccani Dictionary). In short, tourism refers to the set of activities that enable the tourist experience resulting from the temporary transfer to a new place.

At the core of tourism are the transfer from one place to another and the journey that makes this transfer possible. According to Giovanni Boccaccio in 1348, traveling is nothing more than "a more or less long tour through places and countries other than one's own, with stops and stays of various lengths, to see, get to know, learn, have fun." This concise but complete definition accents the purpose of traveling, highlighting its value as a tool for seeing, knowing, learning, and having fun. This perspective is consistent with Omar Khayyam's philosophy that "Life is a journey and who travels lives twice."

C. Baccarani (✉) · D. Cavallo
University of Verona, Verona, Italy
e-mail: claudio.baccarani@univr.it

F. Cassia et al. (eds.), *Accessible Tourism in the Digital Ecosystem*,
SpringerBriefs in Applied Sciences and Technology,
https://doi.org/10.1007/978-3-031-38782-1_6

Through these definitions and statements, we can grasp the ethical value of making the travel experience possible for every person who wishes to live it, regardless of the possible fragility or inconvenience they may feel.

Not all inconveniences can be overcome, but everything possible should be done to remove the obstacles that hinder those who wish to do so from seizing this opportunity. Development in this arena is sustained by the incessant technological progress that enables advancements that seemed unobtainable until recently, such as an artificial-intelligence-supported backpack for blind individuals that enables them to move more easily.

What we have described so far is the ideal condition that should be characteristic of the tourist industry. However, real life clearly reveals a different picture in which journeys often appear as an obstacle race not only for those with disabilities but also for those without.

Anyone who has traveled knows all too well the innumerable problems that can be encountered along the tourism journey from the moment one leaves one's residence until returning home again, thanks to the involvement of multiple stages and actors. There are many obstacles that can materialize, including the selection of the travel destination and available means of transport, the different accommodation options at the chosen destination, and access to the services designed for tourists.

Such difficulties often derive from the fact that the various actors involved in this process do not operate according to a network logic and they do not show systemic relationships, unless they are observed from a distance. In reality, the tourism sector exhibits the traits of a constellation more than those of a system. Observing the sector from afar seems to reveal, like the constellations, connections between the bodies that compose it. When looking at it more closely, we discover that the subjects are very distant from each other, often without network relationships. Actions are driven by individualism and have only low levels of coordination, if any. This situation proves particularly problematic for people who experience some condition of more or less serious discomfort.

Digital platforms are certainly of great technology to solve the mentioned problems since they can facilitate the harmony of relationships among those involved in organizing the trip and in the tourist's stay at the destination. In addition, regulations designed by legislative bodies at both the national and supranational levels certainly facilitate progress toward accessibility in travel and tourism.

But the goal of truly accessible tourism from a perspective of equal dignity of people cannot be achieved without *a collective disposition toward welcoming* by all the tourism operators, local authorities, and the resident population of tourist destinations. Such a disposition goes beyond acting in a perspective of mere hospitality—that is limiting oneself to taking care of the set of technical proposals aimed at responding to the needs of travel and staying at the destination—but should embrace the principles of welcoming and use them to inform actions.

Indeed, welcoming means receiving or accepting someone, consistent with the Latin word *colligere* (composed of *co* and *legere*), meaning gathering together, gathering close to oneself, or hosting with shows of affection. Welcoming indicates attention, care, openness, and sharing something of one's own, such as spaces and places, albeit temporarily.

Hospitality is the basic component of welcoming; the component that is offered as a simple service by those who work in the tourism sector. Welcoming is much more than hospitality because not only is it offered empathetically by operators, but also by individual citizens who help tourists to solve both small and large problems and to experience their journey intensely by immersing themselves in the culture of their destination.

Such an attitude places tourists at the center of attention not as customers, but as people who are enriched through the beauty that the places reveal, but also, and above all, through the immersion in the culture and life of the place, which can rightly be defined as the "travel experience."

In this perspective, a mutual enrichment takes place among tourists, local populations, and operators, who form a temporary community that acts collectively to generate and spread well-being to those who temporarily live in that specific reality.

Welcoming is not a technical output that can somehow be bought, however. Instead, it is a cultural fruit, a way of being that is based on widespread values including listening, dialogue, respect, trust, and empathy that stand as the pillars of accessible tourism. These values, together with the necessary technical skills, should be owned by sector operators and communities to achieve a level of service quality that exceeds travelers' expectations, reaching a so-called unexpected or dream quality. Operators should also focus on the ability to deal with the unpredictability of situations, which any traveler may find an inconvenience to encounter, but especially those facing accessibility difficulties.

Welcoming is proposed as an opportunity to grow through embracing diversity, whether it is connected to the fragility of the subjects or to the nature of people who are different and unique, and the synergies resulting from that diversity.

Starting at the beginning, with responsibilities shared by sector organizations and local authorities, travelers could be provided with: timely transport, equipped with services for people with disabilities; squares and streets without barriers and equipped with audible pedestrian crossings; tactile paving and street furniture that includes benches for the temporary rest of those who, even if only because they are elderly, are unable to walk long distances; gardens with fragrant plants that allow places to be recognized even without being able to see them; signs in tactile languages; public operators able to communicate with the most widespread languages; restaurateurs who promote and reveal the local gastronomic culture rather than simply selling lunches and dinners; and hotel operators who reveal the hidden and often invisible beauties of places. Other signs of welcoming include scooters properly parked along roadsides after use, not abandoned without care across sidewalks; squares and paths without rubbish on the ground; walkways on the beach allowing individuals to reach the sea with a wheelchair; charging stations for batteries of those same wheelchairs placed in the pedestrian paths; and citizens who stop to ask: "are you lost?" or "do you want me to take a picture?" or "do you need help?".

In short, the goal is a place for everyone, perhaps a place on a "Neverland," that can be discovered through traveling and inventing. Achieving this goal is perhaps possible by inventing a true smart tourism that does not "speak" in only technical and artificial words, but is characterized as "humanistic tourism."

The manufacturer's authorised representative in the EU is Springer Nature Customer Service Centre GmbH, Europaplatz 3, 69115 Heidelberg, Germany. If you have any concerns regarding our products, please contact ProductSafety@springernature.com

Printed and bound by CPI Group (UK) Ltd, Croydon, CR0 4YY
02/10/2026
02226885-0002